THE GALLDORA OMNIBUS

THE GALLDORA OMNIBUS

by MODWENA SEDGWICK

illustrated by DIANA JOHN

HARRAP LONDON

PUBLISHER'S NOTE

This volume contains the thirteen favourite stories from *The Adventures of Galldora, The New Adventures of Galldora,* and *A Rag Doll called Galldora,* together with nine new stories.

First published in Great Britain 1973
by GEORGE G. HARRAP & CO. LTD
182–184 High Holborn, London WC1V 7AX

ISBN 0 245 51935 1

Printed by The Anchor Press Ltd, Tiptree, Essex
Made in Great Britain

FOREWORD

I first met Galldora in the summer of 1953. She lay at first unnoticed in a pile of manuscripts on my desk. It was typical of her, of course, not to push herself forward. She is a humble, gentle creature, and the last thing she would think of would be to attract anyone's attention. However, in due course her turn came, and the moment we had read the first story, we knew that here was a new star in her own right. It fell to me, and to my friend and colleague "Jo" (Josephine Plummer), to introduce Galldora to the world of Children's Hour, and on Monday, June 8, there was broadcast Galldora's first adventure: *The Wood Beyond.* Since then something like twenty-seven more adventures have been read over the air, and many of these you will find in the pages which follow. I hope they will give you as much pleasure to read as they have given us and the many thousands of listeners who have already heard them. Galldora, the little rag doll with the black shoe-button eyes, the faded print-dress, and the mouth sewn on in scarlet wool—how glad she must be to see herself at last in a book. "Magic!" I think she would say. "It's magic! Oh, yes! It's the best place of all."

"DAVID"

DAVID DAVIS

Formerly Head of Children's Hour, B.B.C.

CONTENTS

Galldora and the Small Reward

GALLDORA WAS A RAG DOLL, just a home-made rag doll, with shoe-button eyes and a sewn-on mouth and black wool hair, but though she was home-made, Galldora could laugh and sing and cry, in doll fashion, just as well as any other doll. One day Marybell, the little girl who owned Galldora, came into the nursery and said:

"Darling dolls and teddies, I've got a new pram, and I'm going to take you all out for a ride."

The dolls and teddies were delighted, and so was the small stuffed cat. In fact everyone in the nursery was pleased except Galldora. Poor Galldora sat on the window-sill with her head bowed very low, for she felt sure she would be left out of the treat. After all, she was just a home-made rag doll, and prams were very grand. Then, to her great surprise, Marybell picked her up and said: "You are coming too,

Galldora; you look as if you could do with some fresh air, you look a little pale."

Me—me! thought Galldora, as she was pushed into the bottom of the pram. Me! Fancy not being left out after all! She was so thrilled that she hardly noticed what a squash there was in the pram as doll after doll and large and small teddy bears came piling in on top of her.

"Could you squeeze down a bit, Galldora?" a teddy bear said, quite kindly, and a large plastic doll said:

"I might be rather heavy on your leg, Galldora, but I'm afraid that's where I'll have to sit—there's nowhere else."

"That's all right," answered Galldora. She was in such a state of excitement. "Me—Galldora—in a pram!" she kept on saying to herself. Of course, she didn't see much because she was right at the very bottom, with all the dolls and the teddies on top of her keeping out the view, but she knew she was going along in the pram because she was jolted and bumped. Then there was an extra-large bump, and—and nothing.

"Help!" squeaked Bobo, the stuffed cat. "I don't like this at all." The extra-large bump had bumped Galldora sideways, and there she lay, quite comfortably, staring with one eye up at the chinks of blue sky that showed through the arms and legs and ears and clothes of the dolls and teddies on top of her.

"Oh, help!" the stuffed cat kept repeating in a very tiny little dry voice. "Oh, help!"

"Why, what's the matter?" asked Galldora.

"We're in the middle of a stream, and it's most awfully full of water, and, as everybody knows, water's very bad for cats."

"Are we sinking?" asked Galldora. She was quite unafraid, and merely interested.

"If we don't move very much," said the big teddy, "we'll be all right; the pram will be like a boat."

"The water's running past us, and it's making me feel dizzy," sighed Lulu, the walkie-talkie doll. "I feel ever so dizzy, ever so dizzy."

"But why are we here?" asked Galldora.

"Well," said a small white bear, "Marybell said the river would give the pram a nice wash, and she's gone off and left us. She's gone back for a scrubbing-brush and some soap, which she forgot."

Oh, well, I suppose she will come back, thought Galldora, and she stayed peacefully at the bottom of the pram, staring at the chinks of blue sky, and humming little tunes to herself. All the other dolls and teddies chatted away and tried to help Lulu get over her dizzy feeling, and the stuffed cat to get over his nerves. But Marybell didn't come back. She had forgotten all about the new pram. She had run off to play with her very best friend, Gay, and she stayed a long time with Gay, swinging on Gay's swing. Then she went home to tea, and it was not until she was splashing about in her bath that she remembered her pram. The splashing reminded her.

As soon as she remembered she grew very silent. She was so silent after her bath and so very silent during her supper that at last her mummy asked: "What is the matter, Marybell?"

"It's got lost," said Marybell, not quite knowing what to say.

"What has, Marybell?" asked her mother.

"My new pram," said Marybell. "It's got lost in the stream," and that was all Marybell would say.

"But how could it get lost?" asked her mother. "And when did it get lost?"

"It got lost while it was having a wash in the stream," said Marybell. "It's got lost in the stream."

At last Marybell's mother went down to the stream to have a look, and she found the pram, lying on its side, right in the water, with the weeds and the tadpoles all floating in and about it. She pulled the pram out and set it upright, and then she fished about with a long stick and rescued all the teddies and the dolls that she could find.

"Well, I suppose that's the lot of you," said Marybell's mother, as she bundled them into the very wet pram, "there doesn't seem to be any more." As she spoke she trod on something soft. It was the stuffed cat. So she picked up the stuffed cat and put it into the pram with the others, and then had another good look round. There were no dolls, no teddies to be seen anywhere, just water and fish and weeds and green grass and king-cups and reeds. "Well, home we go," said Marybell's mother, and she pushed the dolls and the teddies and the stuffed cat home again. But Galldora was not in the pram. Galldora was a mile away, floating quite happily down the stream.

I am very thankful to that cow for bumping into the pram, thought Galldora, for this is really very nice. On and on floated Galldora down the stream in the golden evening. She watched the green fields slip past her and she watched the swallows as they darted low over the waters, seeking flies to eat. Now, this, thought Galldora, is one of the nicest ways of travelling. Of course, it's a bit wet, and I don't suppose the water will do my stuffing any good, but one can't expect everything. I really think it's even nicer than the pram-ride.

Away and away went the rag doll, with her red dress billowing out like a float about her, and her black wool hair streaming behind. Sometimes her head was under the water, and then she could be friendly with the fishes, and sometimes her head bobbed up over the water, and then she could have polite conversation with the dragonflies and the gnats. I wonder if this will go on for ever and ever? she thought. I really won't mind if it does.

But suddenly she was swilled round in a little eddy of water as it flowed swiftly from under a low iron bridge. The waters whirled her and some floating sticks up against great, smooth stones. To Galldora's surprise, there she stopped. Well, thought Galldora, I suppose I could be in a worse place—and now that I am quite jammed up against these stones, with the sticks all about me, it's not so likely that I will sink.

All that night Galldora stayed there, and she was quite happy, watching the stars and listening to the owls. It's all like a lesson, she told herself, like being educated.

Next day she found she did not lack for company. She was visited by an inquisitive trout who had a nibble at her shoes, and then a toad came and hopped all over her, and decided she made a very nice sun-bathing place. Then a thrush came and had a tug at her eyes, thinking they were small snails, and later a cocky little chaffinch came and asked: "May I please, rag doll, have a piece of your nice hair? It will just do for my nest."

"Certainly," said Galldora, "just help yourself." The chaffinch did. He came back time and

time again, and worried at her hair till she wondered if she would have any hair left. Thinking of nests, Galldora sighed, just one or two sighs, in a homesick way. I wonder, she began to think, if I will ever see all the teddy bears and dolls again, and my own special window-sill?

When the sun was high in the heavens a fisherman came walking along the river path, and stopped on the bridge. He leant there for a moment, gazing down at the cool, clear waters, and wondering about the fish. As he looked his eye was caught by a piece of red-coloured cloth, all muddled up in the pile of driftwood against the big stones and the reeds. He went over and kicked it, in a wondering sort of way, with the toes of his boots. The red-coloured rag was, of course, Galldora, and the kick made her legs and arms leap about.

"Well, well," said the fisherman, "a rag doll." He bent down and picked Galldora out of the water and he wrung her out and he set her up on an iron spike on the railings of the bridge. "I suppose some little girl will be looking for you," said the fisherman, and being a kind fisherman he arranged Galldora very comfortably. He put the spike through the back of her dress and through the back part of her woolly hair, so that her face was right up, and she looked straight out and could watch all that was happening. Then the fisherman tucked her arms one into the other, so they didn't dangle down. Galldora thought the fisherman was the kindest person she had ever met. He had certainly taken a lot of trouble over her. She stayed there on the railings in the sun, smiling out on the world as she dried.

It was a lovely, all-alone place where Galldora was, and it was full of overhanging green trees and mossy banks. The primroses shone there like stars, and, of course, it was just the place where birds felt very at home. So at home that they were all crowded up, and the nests were just everywhere. One lady robin, who had found all the holes and crevices already full of other birds' nests, came flying over to the bridge, and perched there, looking about for a home. As her bright, beady eyes were flickering this way and that, they met Galldora's bright, shoe-button eyes.

"Oh, dear, you do look worried," said Galldora.

"Yes, I am," said the lady robin, "very worried."

"What is the matter?" asked Galldora.

"Well, it's this way," explained the lady robin, "I can't find anywhere to make my nest. Everywhere is full up this year."

"Oh, could I—well, if you didn't think I was interfering—make a suggestion?" said Galldora timidly. The lady robin cocked her head on one side to listen. "You see my arms?" said Galldora. "They are tucked up, aren't they?"

"Yes," said the lady robin.

"Well," said Galldora, still very timidly, "come and have a closer look." The lady robin flew over and, perching on Galldora's head, looked at Galldora's tucked-up arms.

"Why!" said the lady robin, "what a wonderful cosy place to make a nest. It's just what I'm looking for," and she flew away and came back a little later with her husband. At once they started to build a nest in Galldora's arms.

Now, some days later, the fisherman passed Marybell's house. Outside, on a little tree, he saw a notice hanging by some string, and the notice said: LOST—A RAG DOLL. LOST IN RIVER. IF FOUND, SMALL REWARD. He at once rang the bell and told Marybell's mother all about Galldora.

So, that afternoon, Marybell and her mother went down to the lonely, greeny part of the river where very few people went, except fishermen, and there, on the bridge, just as they had been told, they found Galldora. There too they found in Galldora's arms a nest with four eggs.

Marybell's mother, who understood all about eggs and nests, took Marybell a little way away,

and they both sat very silent on the river bank and watched. Quite soon the lady robin came flying straight to Galldora and sat in the nest. Marybell was so excited she wanted to jump up and pick up the eggs, but her mother said:

"No, Marybell, you will upset her, but we'll come every day to see the robin." So every day Marybell came and looked at Galldora and the robins, from a safe distance, of course, so as not to upset the robins. And every day, when she left, Marybell waved her hand at Galldora. And every day Galldora seemed to wink back.

Marybell was so proud of Galldora she said: "You know, Mummy, I think Galldora is the cleverest of all my dolls. I think she must have the small reward that the fisherman didn't want." So Galldora, when the baby robins had grown up and flown away, and she had come home, was given the small reward, which was a diamond star brooch out of a cracker. And Galldora proudly wears it, even to this day.

Galldora and the Scarecrow

THERE WAS ONE GOOD thing about Galldora, Marybell's rag doll; she had been lost so many times, and had found herself in so many strange places, that she had learned a great deal about people and the wide world. Whenever Galldora got very lost and rather frightened, she would bite back her tears, and console herself by thinking, This will be good for my education. Because, as Galldora knew, "a doll's got to have something, and if she hasn't good looks education is useful."

Galldora would not have passed any exams, for her idea of education was quite different from a teacher's, or even Marybell's. For one thing, she couldn't add up two and two; she always thought two and two made ten. No matter how often Marybell would say: "Listen, Galldora, two and two makes four," it made no difference. Galldora would listen but not believe it. She would stare back at Marybell with her shoe-button eyes in dumb silence—almost in a huffy silence. Marybell would know perfectly well what was going on in Galldora's mind. It was this:

"Two and two makes ten. Marybell can think it makes four, but I know it makes ten." Also, Galldora never quite believed in the names given to days, like Monday, Tuesday, and so on; to her it was just yesterday, to-day, and to-morrow.

"Monday, Tuesday, Wednesday," Marybell would say encouragingly, and she would put her face very close to Galldora's sewn-on lips, and Marybell was sure, each time, she could hear Galldora whispering very, very faintly to herself:

"Yesterday, to-day, and to-morrow. . . ."

"Oh, dear!" Marybell would say, "you are a very clever doll in your own way, I know, Galldora, but it's nobody else's way."

Now one day Galldora got very, very lost. She was left lying on a flowering bank at the edge of a great, wide field. It happened like this. Marybell and Galldora had gone out for a walk with Marybell's mother to pick cowslips. Galldora had been put down very gently for just a moment, while Marybell ran on ahead to gather some very tall cowslips that were dangling so beautifully. "Oh, Mummy, Mummy!" Marybell had cried, "There's ten bells on this one—do come and look!" Marybell's mummy got up from her nice resting-place on the bank by Galldora, and went to look at the cowslip. No sooner had Marybell's mummy come up to her than Marybell ran farther on and called: "Mummy! Come quickly, there's a larger one here; it has so many bells I can't count them all at once." So, on and on they went from flower to flower, for each year they always tried to find the cowslip with the most bells. One year Marybell's mother had found one with fifteen bells.

Marybell will come back for me, thought Galldora, as she lay among the mosses and the violets, but Marybell didn't. Both Marybell and her mummy soon had their hands full of cowslips, so full that they went home quickly to arrange them in jam-jars for the nursery and kitchen before the gay yellow flowers wilted from being held too tightly. They didn't even remember Galldora when they got home. They were too busy arranging the flowers. Then Marybell wanted to press some, which meant finding blotting-paper and heavy books. Yes, they were so busy and happy that neither of them gave Galldora a thought.

Poor Galldora lay on her back for hours and hours. She watched the colour of the sky change from sunny blue to a deep pink, edged with gold, and then to the deep, dark, clear blue

of a fine night sky. Galldora could see a slim new moon, very white and shivery.

There's an awful lot of sky for it to float about on, thought Galldora. I wonder how it knows its way? There was one bright star by the moon, and it seemed more lost and shivery than the moon. The moon floated up and up into the sky and it dragged the little star along behind it. Very clever of the moon to know its way, thought Galldora, for there's no signpost or anything up there. An owl, looking like a great white moth, swooped so near Galldora that she cried: "Oh! I do wish you would make some noise as you fly, owl. You gave me quite a start." The owl passed backward and forward several times. "You startle me every time," gasped Galldora. "Why don't you wear squeaky wings, or something?" The owl hovered above for a moment and, ignoring such a silly remark, asked:

"Are you hiding a mouse?"

"Certainly not!" said Galldora, with as much dignity as she could, for it was rather difficult to be dignified and haughty, while lying flat on your back. The owl went away and after a time a big brown, ragged field-mouse came scuttering up from the ditch and sat very close to Galldora. It started to clean its whiskers. Then the mouse, noticing Galldora, nodded its head and said, politely: "Nice night," and went on its way.

That was a most polite mouse, thought Galldora. After a few hours several hares came and frisked about. Then they formed a circle while two hares in the middle had a boxing match. And as the two hares boxed, the others chanted:

"There was a man of double deed
Sowed his garden full of seed.
When the seed began to grow,
'Twas like a garden full of snow;
When the snow began to melt,
'Twas like a ship without a belt;
When the ship began to sail,
'Twas like a bird without a tail;
When the bird began to fly,
'Twas like an eagle in the sky;
When the sky began to roar,
'Twas like a lion at the door;
When the door began to crack——"

Then suddenly, as if all the hares were tired of the game at once, they broke the circle and hurried away.

What frightened them? Galldora wondered, but she never knew.

As the whisper of dawn moved among the sleepy violets, a hawk came out and sat upon a bare high pine-tree. He was as grey as the dawn at first, but as the sun warmed in the sky, so the hawk took on a pinkish richer colour. He saluted the sun in his own fashion, then flew off. All the small birds, led by the robin and the blackbird, had started their morning prayers. No sooner had they finished than a crowd of baby rabbits came to play about the field. They all stood in a line, and one larger rabbit stood in front of them and pointing to each rabbit in turn he said:

"Hana, mana, mona, mike,
Barcelona, bona, strike,
Hare, ware, frown, venac,
Harrico, warrico, we, wo, wac."

Each time he came to "Wac," a rabbit fell out of the line.

"He is counting them out," said Galldora, watching; and on and on went the big rabbit, saying ever faster and faster:

"Hana, mana, mona, mike,
Barcelona, bona, strike,
Hare, ware, frown, venac,
Harrico, warrico, we, wo, wac."

until there was only one rabbit left, and he at once set about running and catching the others.

Soon a church bell began to toll. It sounded so homely to Galldora that she almost cried.

"They'll soon come for me now," said Galldora, "for the bell means every one is awake and going to church." But no one came for Galldora—no Marybell, no Marybell's mother, no one at all.

Two days later Galldora was found by a man

who had come to harrow the large field. He picked her up and took her to the middle of the field. He stuck a great stake in the ground, and he put Galldora on the top of the stake by tying her to it with a piece of string. Then he went away. He came back later with a large, real scarecrow, and he set the scarecrow up by the rag doll.

"There you are," he said. "There's company for you both." He tied some queer string all about Galldora, and another about the scarecrow. Then he took out a box of matches and lit the ends of both the strings. Then he went again across the field.

Galldora peeped at the scarecrow and the scarecrow looked away and took no notice, though Galldora could see that he was rather pleased that he was being stared at. Suddenly there was a bang, and Galldora gave a great jump and said, "Oh!" A little later there was another bang, and it came from the scarecrow. But the scarecrow didn't go "Oh!" He just stood with his arms out, staring across the field to a distant spinney.

"What were those bangs?" asked Galldora.

"New-fangled notions," said the scarecrow, "I don't hold with new-fangled notions."

"Don't you?" said Galldora, very pleased that the scarecrow had at last slightly turned his head and had spoken to her.

"What, me?" said the scarecrow. "Me hold with new-fangled notions?"

"Sometimes new things are very good," said Galldora. She was just saying anything that came into her head so as to keep the conversation going.

"I don't hold with anything new," snapped the scarecrow, "but that's hardly surprising, seeing I come from an ancient family."

"Do you?" said Galldora brightly. What a nice conversation we are having, she thought.

"Very ancient," went on the scarecrow, "so ancient that the first scarecrows are lost backward into the dawn of history. My family and man's family grew up together, you might say, side by side. But sometimes I think my family was afore man's," boasted the scarecrow.

"Oh, but that can't possibly be," said Galldora, "because who could have made the first scarecrows if there were no humans to make them?" The scarecrow swung round in the breeze and gave Galldora a long stare.

"I can see you're not h'educated," he said.

"Oh, yes—but I am!" said Galldora. "Very

educated. I know that two and two make ten, and I know the days of the week. They are: yesterday, to-day, and to-morrow." Marybell would have been very ashamed of Galldora saying such stupid things, but it impressed the scarecrow, who turned away and sulked. There was another bang, and Galldora went: "Hiccup!" Then the scarecrow banged, and said:

"Not much use, these bangs, if you ask me."

"I didn't ask you," said Galldora, "but I will. Aren't they any use?"

"No, never," said the scarecrow. "Now, I knows my work, but them humans thinks I don't, see? I scare away the crows and rooks and jackdaws when I wants to—that is, not afore I wants to, you understand; and not after I wants to, you understand—but when I wants to."

"But these bangs," said Galldora, feeling a little muddled, "do they scare away the birds?"

"New-fangled notions!" was all the scarecrow answered. "Never did hold with new-fangled notions."

Just then a huge flock of rooks came swirling down into the field, like bits of scattered paper. They settled to peck and eat quite happily. Some jackdaws had joined them, but kept up high for a while, and tumbled over and about each other as they flew, until Galldora laughed. "Clowns," was all the scarecrow said, as he too watched them. He said "Clowns" in a very disapproving way. Then came two pairs of lapwings, with a "Pee-wit, pee-wit." "Ha! So they're back again," said the scarecrow.

"Why? Don't they usually come?" asked Galldora.

"Not usually in these parts," answered the scarecrow, and Galldora was so impressed with the scarecrow's knowledge that she wondered if she ought to call him 'sir' in future. But she wasn't so sure about his cleverness a little later on when two crows came and sat on his arm. They sat there just talking, and not a bit scared of him.

"It was a big worm," said one.

"Ah!" said the other, "Ah—ah!"

Why doesn't he scare them away? thought Galldora. Then one of her bangers went bang very loudly, and the two crows flew off. Galldora called out with joy: "I've done it! I've done it! I've done it! It was me." But then Galldora stopped. Oh, dear! she didn't want to offend the scarecrow. "You should have——" she began.

"I does when I wants to, and I don'ts when

I don't," said the scarecrow, in a very cross voice, "and I'd like you to mind your own

business." A loud bang went off by his trailing coat, and he shook a little with rage.

Suddenly the whole flock of blackbirds, rooks, jackdaws, and crows came all round them. They were very familiar and sat on the scarecrow's arms and hat, and even on Galldora.

Galldora thought: I do wish that scarecrow would shoo away the birds. I'm feeling quite faint, they are so heavy. But the scarecrow seemed to be taking no notice. I suppose he's in one of his "I-don't-when-I-don't" moods, thought Galldora. Then, suddenly, all her bangers went off together. The noise was terrific, and the birds, with a loud clap of wings, flew away all at once. But the bangers had set fire to the string that tied Galldora to the stake, and she fell to the ground. The birds came back. They stamped over Galldora in a most vulgar way.

"Oh, please, Mr Scarecrow—do something!" begged Galldora. The scarecrow took no notice. Galldora was so trodden-on that she was very afraid she would be trodden into the soft, new-harrowed earth, and then she would never be found. I think that scarecrow is just a sham, thought Galldora to herself. Then, suddenly, the scarecrow swung round and round on his stick, and he shouted:

"I'll shoot the wren on Christmas morning!" It worked like magic. The birds flew away, and didn't come back.

"Thank you," said Galldora limply, but her faint voice was lost, as the wind had suddenly got up and was raging over the young corn, and with it came a drift of cold, spring snow. There Galldora lay, all snowed over and muddy. The next day a hot sun came up, and dried the whole field, and Galldora.

"Hello!" called the scarecrow, "are you there?"

"Yes," said Galldora weakly, "just about, I think, but I don't feel very like myself."

"I feel fine," called down the scarecrow, "but then, I come from an ancient family that stretches back to the dawn of the world. Afore man we scarecrows were. Now, answer me this riddle. I'm in a mood for fun and games." The scarecrow seemed to be in great good humour.

I don't want to. I only want to be found, sadly thought Galldora, but she listened politely.

"White bird featherless
 Flew from Paradise,
Pitched on the castle wall;
 Along came Lord Landless,
 Took it up handless,
And rode away horseless to the
 King's white hall,"

said the scarecrow.

And even before Galldora had time to try and think of the answer the scarecrow shouted:

"Snow and sun is the answer, and I bet you could not have thought of that answer in a hundred years from now, but we scarecrows know all the answers and snow and sun."

Two men came across the field. "Hello!" said the farmer, looking down at Galldora. "Looks to me like the rag doll that belongs to Marybell. How on earth did you come here?"

"I put she up as a scarecrow," explained the man who had harrowed the field, "but she don't seem no good, not like the old scarecrow she don't."

"There! What did I tell you?" whispered the scarecrow to Galldora as she was lifted up. "We scarecrows are born, not made. We go back to the dawn of history, afore man."

Galldora only thought of all the answers she would have liked to have given to that proud scarecrow after she was back in her own nursery, warm and dry and patched. "Anyway," she consoled herself, "I know that two and two makes ten, and that silly old scarecrow didn't."

Galldora's Birthday Present

GALLDORA HAD BEEN GIVEN to Marybell by her favourite uncle, Uncle Jack, as an unbirthday present. This made it very difficult for Marybell to remember Galldora's birthday. Some of the dolls and teddies had their birthdays on Christmas Day, which was a proper sort of day to have a birthday on, while the other dolls and teddies had their birthdays on the same day as Marybell's. That day was easy to remember, and they all had a share of Marybell's birthday cake. But Marybell did get a bit muddled trying to remember Galldora's birthday.

So sometimes on a bright summer's day Marybell would say: "It's your birthday to-day, Galldora," and sometimes Galldora had a birthday in November. Some years she had two birthdays. But other years Galldora didn't have a birthday at all.

"I don't mind a bit not having a birthday,"

Galldora would say to herself, "for if I did have two birthdays every year I think I'd be a very old doll by now. Not having birthdays every now and again keeps one young."

One cold winter's day Marybell said: "To-morrow, Galldora, it's your birthday." Galldora smiled at Marybell.

"Oh, how lovely, that would be very nice."

"It's got to be to-morrow and not to-day," explained Marybell, "because there's a lot of preparing to do."

Preparing? thought Galldora. That sounds as if it's going to be a proper birthday.

All that day Marybell polished up the nursery and washed and scrubbed the dolls. She brushed the teddies, and tied bright ribbons on them all. The teddies all had blue ribbons tied in beautiful bows round their necks, because they were boys, and the dolls all had pink ribbons in their hair, because they were girls: while the stuffed cat had a yellow ribbon tied round his middle, as Marybell could never make up her mind whether the stuffed cat was a boy or a girl.

"Oh, dear," suddenly said Marybell, when she came to Galldora, "I haven't any ribbons left. Still, perhaps it doesn't matter. As it's your birthday, Galldora dear, you can come to the tea-party just as you are."

Before Marybell went to bed, she arranged all

the dolls and teddies and the stuffed cat on the window-seat. They looked so smart, brushed and washed, and their ribbons looked very gay. Galldora, as it was Galldora's birthday, she left on the window-sill, just above them. "There," said Marybell, "now we are all ready for Galldora's birthday to-morrow. How nice you all look, and Bobo, I've never seen you looking so well and smart. I think that yellow ribbon round your middle makes you look very handsome. Now, good-night, all of you, and to-morrow we'll have lovely fun, for it's Galldora's birthday, remember." The nursery door closed softly, and Marybell went to bed.

After a while, there was a soft whisper among the toys on the window-seat. It was like the soft rustling of wind among the winter trees. Galldora was suddenly aware that the dolls and teddies were whispering about her.

"Galldora's so kind I'm sure she's thought of a present for us," said Lulu, the walkie-talkie doll.

"Yes, she is so clever," said Bobo. "I am sure she's thought up a wonderful present for us all."

"Galldora is the only one that could think up a present, she's got such a lot of brains," said the Baby Doll.

"Dear Galldora, she's so old and wise," the White Teddy softly growled.

Me! thought Galldora. They are talking about

me, and they are thinking all those nice things about me. But I haven't thought of any present to give them. It's *my* birthday—but still, yes, it would be nice to give them all a present on my birthday.

Soon their whisperings grew fainter and fainter, and Galldora could only catch a whisper that sounded like: "Marybell thought up a wonderful present for me to give Galldora. It is . . ."

"That's the big Teddy," said Galldora, to herself. "He never could speak softly." Then she heard Alouetta say, in her chirpy way: "Marybell wrapped my present to Galldora in silver paper. It makes it look better as it's so little, but fun."

Oh, dear! thought poor Galldora, how can I open all my presents and say thank you when I haven't got anything for them, and they're all expecting one. It's going to be a very muddled-up birthday.

Silence fell in the nursery. All the toys were asleep except Galldora. I must think of something, thought Galldora. It's all so still. I'm sure that's good for thinking. But oh! if only some magic would happen. If only I had a magic wand. But I'm no fairy, only a rag doll.

Still, if I wished and wished——Galldora made herself quite dizzy with wishing.

But though Galldora had no magic wand there was magic in the night. It was Marybell's mother who started the magic. She came into the nursery and put Galldora's presents on the table. Then Marybell's mother came over to the window. "We must have a little air," she said, "It's very stuffy in here, but I know Marybell will be very upset if I move any of the dolls and teddies." So she opened the window by Galldora. "There," she said, "that's better. Nice, clean air," and with that she went away.

It grew so cold the stars began to sing to the moon to warm themselves up. And they sang together: "Moon bright, moon light, please bring snow to-night."

Then the moon smiled and said, "That would be fun," and called to the winds: "Wind East, wind North, bring snow forth."

The winds blew, and soon the sky was full of dancing, falling snowflakes. They fell through the half-open window and on to Galldora.

The snow blew all over Galldora until she could hardly see for snow. It covered her wool hair, it covered her face till her shoe-button eyes could only peep out. It covered her shoulders, then her whole body, and it filled her lap. It piled up higher and higher, and still the wind blew. By early morning, Galldora was so covered by snow that she suddenly toppled over, and as she fell clouds of the snow floated

on all the dolls and teddies, till each of them had enough snow on their paws, or on their legs or on their dresses to make for each of them a little snowball. Galldora lay on the floor, face downward. She was so tired with thinking about what to give them all as a present that she went fast asleep.

Next morning Marybell came into the nursery. It was still very early, and Marybell was in her dressing-gown. She saw Galldora on the floor.

She picked Galldora up. Galldora looked so wet and sad, and it looked as if her shoe-button eyes had been crying and crying.

"Oh, Galldora," said Marybell, "you musn't cry to-day, it's your birthday." Then Marybell saw the snow on the other dolls and teddies. "Why, Galldora," she said, "I believe you've put it there. You've given them all a present," and Marybell made of the snow a little snow-ball for each of them. When she had finished she woke them up and said: "Listen, dolls and teddies. Galldora's been so kind. As it's her birthday she's given you all a present of a snowball each." The dolls and teddies were terribly excited, and looked at their snowballs with delight.

"Oh, thank you, Galldora," they cried. "What a nice present! We knew you were clever and kind, and would think up something lovely, but this is really like magic."

So my wish came true, Galldora thought. Though I had no magic some one must have had to magic up the snow. Galldora had an extra-happy birthday.

Galldora and the Big Fish

ONE DAY MARYBELL SAID to Galldora: "We're going on a very important fishing expedition, Galldora. Uncle Jack is going in for a fishing competition, and you and I are going with him to help him win the prize."

So the party of Marybell, Galldora, and Uncle Jack, with the picnic-basket, the fishing-rods and tackle, set off. When they came to the river they were given a number and place on the bank. And when a pistol was fired all the fishermen along the river bank started fishing.

But fishing is a slow business and Marybell soon got very bored. She wandered away to pick wild flowers and left Galldora to look after Uncle Jack. Now, Galldora and Uncle Jack knew each other well, for Uncle Jack had made Galldora and so, naturally, he was very fond of the rag doll. He had propped her up kindly against the fishing-basket so that she might look out over the river and watch the moorhens and the wind-ripples on the water. Galldora was very happy; she found just sitting and not thinking a peaceful way of spending your life. I like fishing, she thought.

But, after a lunch, a terrible thing happened. With all the moving of the picnic-baskets and the opening of "Thermos" flasks, neither Uncle Jack nor Marybell noticed that Galldora was jerked from her safe place and slowly, very slowly tumbled head over heels and went—*plomp*—into the water. She lay floating in the river. A swan, one of the two who had come for scraps, made a dive and began to peck at Galldora. She turned over and over and was moved over to the other side of the river—a weedy side. Galldora got stuck in the duck-weed, and entwined with water-violet stems. The water-lily leaves hid her and the tubby yellow water-lily flowers were so like the colour of her frock that none of her family on the bank saw her. Poor Galldora!

When it was time to go home Marybell started to look for Galldora. Galldora was nowhere. Though, of course, she was really so close she could hear Marybell say: "Where can Galldora have got to?" At last, they both gave up searching for her, and went home. Marybell was in tears, and her daddy comforted her by saying she could go back to-morrow and search again, as it was a two-day competition, and he would come and search too. Uncle Jack said nothing, he was too sad—sad at losing Galldora, and sad because he had caught no fish.

Galldora lay face down, her shoe-button eyes bright and wet and shining, her wool hair wild and floating with the weeds, her sewn-on mouth trying to keep firm in the rippling water. "Oh, well," said Galldora bravely, to herself: "I suppose it is better it was me and not Marybell. I must say my rag body seems to be standing up to the water quite well." She didn't like to think further than that. She was not quite sure what would happen to her if she stayed on and on in the river.

Just then a big fish swam right up to Galldora and, looking at her, said: "I'm bigger than you."

"I don't believe you are," said Galldora, indignantly. The fish lashed his tail, and opened and shut his mouth, but he was too cross to say anything for a time. Then he said:

"How dare you contradict me!" And he tried to measure himself against Galldora, but found this very difficult, so he swam away.

Soon the Big Fish came back and this time

with a great many other fish all swimming behind him. "There she is!" shouted the Big Fish crossly. "She says she is bigger than me—ha, ha, ha!" His laugh was rather a dry kind of laugh, more like a cough than a laugh. The little fishes swam all about Galldora and they took little bites at her here and there, and they tweaked at her hair, and they worried her eyes quite terribly.

"Hi!" cried Galldora. "You'll pull my eyes off if you go on."

"You can see for yourself," went on the Big Fish, "she's much smaller than me."

"Well, I like that!" said Galldora. She was getting very cross with this big, boastful bully of a fish. "I am certainly longer than you; I may even be fatter, but I'm not sure of that. Anyway, you're quite horribly fat—you ought to go on a diet."

"Oh, listen to her!" gasped all the little fishes. They were amazed that anyone could talk like that to the Big Fish. The Big Fish goggled his eyes.

"All right," he said, "we'll get properly measured. Take her down to the bottom," he ordered his companions. At once Galldora was seized and the little fishes, all holding on to her here and there, tried to tug her down to the bottom of the river. But they found it too difficult.

I do wish I'd kept quiet, thought Galldora,

but I still think I'm longer than that boastful fish. It will be even more sad for me at the bottom of the river. Uncle Jack and Marybell will never find me there, and I'll be lost for ever.

"Hurry up—hurry up!" shouted the Big Fish.

"She won't come," one little fish piped up. "She's too big."

"Nonsense!" said the Big Fish. "I'll soon get her down," and he swam up and tugged at Galldora's hair.

"OW!" cried Galldora. "Manners, please!" But she felt herself suddenly jerked away from the weeds and slowly, slowly, she was tugged down under the water by all the fishes.

At the bottom of the river she found herself looking up. It was strange to see no sky, no trees, no grass, only water and a few drifting water-lily roots. The little fishes at once bustled about, still tugging and tweaking, and they laid her out flat on a sandy part of the river-bed. Then they tied her hands and her feet and her hair with thin, fibrous roots, and they pegged the roots into the river-bed with little bits of wood. Then they brought hundreds of little pebbles and gravel and put these on her, to make quite sure she would not float up again. After that, the little fishes measured Galldora by placing themselves one behind the other, heads to tails; then they did the same to the Big Fish, and then—then they were silent.

"Well," cried the Big Fish, "I'm the bigger,

aren't I? I'm the biggest fish in the whole river, and the cleverest. She must be taught a lesson. How dare she pretend she's bigger than me!"

The little fishes said nothing.

"Come on—speak up!" shouted the Big Fish.

One of the fishes was pushed forward by the others. He was very nervous.

"Go on—tell him," whispered the others.

"I can't," sobbed the little fish, "I can't." Then the other fishes began to push the little fish, and they edged him forward until he was right under the Big Fish's nose. The little fish blurted out: "She's much longer than you, sir."

"What!" shouted the Big Fish, his bulging eyes flashing. "What did you say, you impertinent little, miserable, come-again, little shivering fish?"

"She's—she's—" stammered the little fish, edging away, "she's longer than you, and larger." The Big Fish rushed at the group of little fishes, and they swam away in a muddle and a bundle and a leaping and scuttling. Galldora was left alone.

All night she stayed there, with the river slowly washing over her, and she couldn't move at all. "It's very peaceful, really," said Galldora to herself, trying to make the most of a very, very sad situation. "There's no wind down here, anyway, and I'll soon get used to it. I'm glad, too, it's a gravelly bit I'm on, and not a muddy bit; and, really, those water-lily roots look very attractive—like gay party streamers." Once or twice the Big Fish came up and glared at Galldora, and said "Ha!" and then went away again.

Morning came, and Galldora still couldn't move. The river washing over her had not dislodged a single speck of gravel. The Big Fish came again and smiled at Galldora in a nasty way.

"So you," he said, "are longer than me. Well, well! But I don't believe you are as clever. Oh, no, I'm the cleverest fish in the whole river." The little fishes came fussing round, listening and peeping; they were very curious.

"Those," sneered the Big Fish, "those are always getting caught. Of course, they get thrown back—it's the law in this part of the river—but it's me the fishermen would really like to catch. I'm the biggest fish in the whole river."

"How do you know?" asked Galldora.

"Because," said the Big Fish, "I've heard those fishermen talking—oh, yes, the real fishermen, the good ones, you know, are all after me. They call me Fred. 'There goes Fred again,' they say. But they can't catch me—ho, ho, ho! I'm much too clever."

Just then, all the little fish began to get very excited. They rushed to the top of the river, and they swam here and there. But the Big Fish was unmoved. He stayed beside Galldora, smiling, and slowly, very slowly waving his tail. "They're baiting," he said.

"Who?" asked Galldora.

"The fishermen."

I wonder who's winning? thought Galldora. Looking up, she noticed that many of the little fishes were caught, one after another. And many of them were thrown back at once, others kept to be weighed before they were put back.

It caused a great deal of squeaking and flurry among them. Suddenly they all swam away, hoping for better food elsewhere. Then another fish, a lazy one, but not as lazy as the Big Fish, came nosing above.

"That's Ted," murmured the Big Fish, "a nice chap, but an awful fool. We'll have a bit of fun now—you watch." Sure enough, Ted very soon swallowed a hook and was whipped up through the waters. The Big Fish roared with laughter.

Oh, good, thought Galldora, I do hope that's Marybell's Uncle Jack's hook. It ought to be; that fish will surely help him win. Then she looked at the very big fish near her. If only—she thought—if only——

"They can't catch me," said the Big Fish, as if he had read her thoughts. "Ho, ho! What a joke to see them whirled up like that. Sometimes I think it is a pity they throw them back again. Hello, here comes Ted again."

Ted was very cross. "Of all the dirty, low-down tricks those humans play, that was the worst! In all my experience—and of experience, I can tell you, I've had a great deal—that was the meanest and nastiest."

"Ho, ho, ho!" laughed the Big Fish. "My

dear chap, your experience can't have taught you much. Why, I could tell that was a hook—I had no doubt at all."

If only, thought Galldora, if only I could get the Big Fish on the hook. A new tasty bit came floating through the water. "There we go again," laughed the Big Fish.

"Is there a hook in there?" asked Galldora.

"Of course," said the Big Fish. Just then, one of the small fish darted near and swallowed the tasty morsel, but there was no hook on it.

"I thought you were the cleverest fish in the river," said Galldora in surprise. The Big Fish glared at her. Another tasty morsel floated by, and the same thing happened. "Well, well," said Galldora, "I believe you're just a fraud, Mr Big Fish, you can't tell when a hook is inside a tasty morsel or not. You are really no cleverer than the other fish."

"Of course I know," snapped the Big Fish; he was very ruffled. Something glittered high up in the sunny fusion of the top waters, and then was gone, but Galldora had seen the hook. "And that," said the Big Fish, "has no hook in it. When it floats back I'll snap it up—you'll see."

"Oh, I shouldn't," said Galldora, kind-heartedly, for she was almost sure there was a hook in the tasty morsel, "you may be wrong."

"Wrong?" shouted the Big Fish. "I'm never wrong."

Suddenly it happened. A glitter, a swish of the tail, and the Big Fish snapped, and was caught. How he lashed in the waters! How he cunningly tried to free himself! But no, he was caught all right, though at one moment Galldora thought he would snap the line with his great weight. But Uncle Jack was a good fisherman, and played him well.

The Big Fish's struggle had surged up the whole river-bed and, to Galldora's surprise, she found herself floating upward.

"Galldora—look, Daddy—Galldora!" cried Marybell.

Marybell's daddy at once took up a boat-hook that he had brought to search for the rag doll and, putting it over the water, hooked up Galldora.

"Mind my line!" Uncle Jack cried. "I've a beauty of a big fish here."

Galldora was saved, and Uncle Jack with the help of the Big Fish won the competition. As the Big Fish was thrown back into the river Galldora called to him:

"Thank you for stirring up the river and setting me free."

"Thank me for nothing," snapped the Big Fish rudely, as he splashed into the water. But he was very pleased Galldora was no longer going to be in the river.

"You know, I think," said Marybell, squeezing out the water from the rag doll, "I think Galldora put that big fish on the hook for you, Uncle Jack."

"I wouldn't be a bit surprised," said Uncle Jack, smiling. Galldora smiled too.

And the sunlight on her wet shoe-button eyes made her give a little wink.

Galldora and the Little Cat

ONE DAY GALLDORA found herself sitting on top of a house. It's a good thing I'm not afraid of heights, she thought, as she sat there propped up against a chimney-stack. The sun blazed, and the green trees stirred very gently, and the whole summery hot, hazy garden spread out below, like a dream. Galldora watched the swallows flying about, and heard them chattering away to themselves and, looking up, she could see the swifts. Miles and miles up they winged, racing each other and screaming with joy. Looking far down, she could see a family of long-tailed tits flying here and there like little wound-up toys.

I suppose, thought Galldora, it must be rather nice to be a bird and fly. If only I could fly all my troubles would be over. I could just fly down on to the lawn.

Just then two wood-pigeons came and sat on the roof beside her. They looked at her with one eye and then with the other. Funny, thought Galldora, they can't look at me with both eyes at once.

A little later, when the sun was dipping and the shadows stretched out and out, Galldora saw the little boy who had thrown her up from the nursery window and on to the roof. He was saying good-bye to his cousin Marybell and to Marybell's mummy and daddy. His own mummy and daddy were with him. They were all laughing and talking and saying, "Good-bye, and thank you for a lovely day," over and over again, or so it seemed to Galldora, who was watching. The little boy did cast a look up at Galldora, a hurried look. I hope, thought poor Galldora, he will say something about me before he goes. But he didn't.

All was peaceful in the garden once again. All the birds, and the sleepy, hot flowers, and the full-leaved trees were happy and all in their right places—all except Galldora.

For sitting on a roof is no place at all for a rag doll, thought Galldora. It's all right for birds, but not for rag dolls. Still, perhaps that little boy didn't mean me to get stuck.

A blackbird came and sat on an old apple-tree in the garden and started up a clear, tuneful evening song. Marybell's mother and Marybell came and tidied up deck-chairs and cushions that were lying on the lawn.

"Listen, Marybell, that blackbird is singing beautifully," and both Marybell and her mother stood for a moment and looked up at the bird and listened.

"If I had a worm I would give it to that blackbird for singing so beautifully," said Marybell. Then, having tidied up the lawn, both Marybell and her mother went back into the house.

The long shadows mingled one with another, and soon the night wind blew a star into the sky. The moon came out to ride her long lone ride in the heavens and see that all was in order, and all the little stars hurried to their places.

This is terribly sad, thought Galldora, and the saddest thing of all is that there is nobody here to know how sad I am.

Just then Galldora's attention was caught by a strange noise—a scratching noise and a faint purr. Then more scratching noises came, then a soft meow. Galldora saw a small furry face coming round the chimney-stack, whiskers first.

"It is a dear little white-and-black cat," said Galldora to herself. "I'm so glad. Now I will have somebody to know how sad I am."

One white paw, then a black paw, came round the stack, and the little cat's shoulders came too. It was creeping silently and cautiously, gazing about with great wide eyes. At first, because Galldora didn't move, it didn't see the rag doll, but as soon as it saw Galldora, the little cat was so startled it nearly fell off the roof.

"It's all right, really, it's all right, it's only me," called Galldora.

"Oh! it's you, is it?" answered the cat. It came and sniffed Galldora, then it looked about, and it whispered: "Where are THEY?"

"Who?" asked Galldora.

"The gang," whispered the little cat. Galldora was just going to say, "What gang?" when she noticed the little cat had gone. Suddenly the little cat appeared round the other side of the chimney-stack, and it whispered: "They are not here yet——"

"Must you be so mysterious?" asked Galldora. "Who is the gang?"

"The gang are the big cats," answered the little cat, speaking very softly, "and I do hope, now that I've managed to climb the roof, they'll let me in on all their secrets. They discuss very important things, you know, but they never let on—well, anyway, not when they're down there. Even if I say 'hello' they look straight through me, really they do—straight through me, as if I was a baby still—and it's most upsetting. But I have climbed the roof now, so—oh! what was that?" suddenly exclaimed the little cat.

An appalling caterwauling had started. The little cat smiled. "That's them," he whispered. "Oh, dear, I do feel all of a quiver."

"If I were you," Galldora started, "I should ask them politely——" but she got no further, for the noise the cats were making was deafening. It grew louder and louder, and then a low whinny started up. The little cat was grinning.

"They're gathering—they're gathering!" he purred, excitedly. "Don't they sing beautifully? Excuse me, I'll go and join them now." Galldora hoped all would be well with the little cat, but there was such a hissing and screaming and snarling and grumbling and fur flying, that Galldora was afraid the big cats had all set on the little cat as soon as they saw him.

Oh, I do hope they don't hurt him, thought Galldora, getting very motherly.

Suddenly the little cat came round the chimney stack again. "Well?" asked Galldora curiously.

"Oh, dear!" gasped the little cat, "it's worse and worse."

"How?" asked Galldora.

"Because," said the little cat, "I've got to answer questions before I can join the gang.

The first one is ever so difficult. I simply don't know what the answer is."

"Well, what's the question?" asked Galldora, and added proudly, "I may be able to help you."

"I hope you can," whispered the cat. "It is: 'What looks with one eye but has two?' "

"Oh, but I know," cried Galldora excitedly.

"Oh, please don't talk so loudly," begged the little cat; "they'll hear you."

"I do know," Galldora whispered. "It's birds."

"Are you sure?" asked the little cat.

"Why, yes," said Galldora, "for two pigeons came and sat on the roof here beside me, this very afternoon. And they could only look at me with one eye at a time, I noticed specially." The little cat said nothing. He licked his paw and then licked round his face. "I know that's right, really I do," said Galldora. "Go on, go and tell them." The little cat still took no notice, then he got up, stretched, and went round the chimney-stack without a word.

A low chanting started from the big cats. This went on for a terribly long time. Then the screeching and hissing started up again. The little cat came back to Galldora. He was looking scared again, but this time there was a little glint of cockiness in his wide, gold eyes.

"Well?" asked Galldora.

"I gave the right answer," was all the little cat said. He might thank me, thought Galldora, but the little cat didn't thank her, he only said: "They asked me another question."

Well, he can jolly well think of the answer for himself, thought Galldora.

"The question was: 'How can you get milk and food from humans?' I said 'I just cry,' but they said that wasn't the right answer."

"Of course it wasn't right," said Galldora, and though she didn't have any intention of helping the little cat, she couldn't help saying: "If I could sing I'd sing, and then my dear Marybell—the girl who owns me, you know—she'd say, 'Why, Galldora, how beautifully you sing,' and she'd give me anything I wanted."

"How do you know?" asked the little cat, sitting very straight and squinting at the moon.

"When the blackbird sang in the garden," went on Galldora, "Marybell looked up at him and said: 'If I had a worm I would give it to that blackbird for singing so beautifully.'"

"Ah!" smiled the little cat.

"But, of course, you can't sing," said Galldora.

"I can purr," answered the little cat, and he padded away over the roof. Galldora listened, but this time no whining or caterwauling happened. The little cat appeared again, very quickly. It sat down and started to try and lick behind its ears.

"I'm not going to talk to that little cat," Galldora told herself, "he's getting more conceited every moment. He can talk to me first if he wants to."

He did—and the little cat said, "I'm getting

very clever at this guessing game." Then he had another lick, and he said, as if it wasn't anything very important, "I've got to answer a third and last question," and the little cat went on licking himself, and Galldora went on being silent. The little cat couldn't get its paws behind its ears, try as it might.

"Ah, so it's not going to rain," said Galldora. She never could keep quiet for long.

"And why do you think that?" asked the little cat, turning his head slightly away.

"Because you haven't licked behind your ears. Cats only lick behind their ears when it's going to rain. That's what Marybell told me, anyway."

"Now I know," said the little cat, and it put its little pink tongue out and licked its black nose. Then it got up, and walked away, with its tail held high in a question-mark.

"Oh, bother!" said Galldora to herself. "I believe that was the answer to the third question. He wanted to know what cats do when it's going to rain." It must have been the right answer to the third question, for all the rest of the night, the little cat sat with the big cats on the far side of the roof, and listened to them discussing high secrets. To Galldora it sounded a terrible noise, and she was quite pleased when a window below her was opened, and Marybell's daddy looked out and shouted: "Shoo! Shoo!" and then clapped his hands. The cats, in a great flurry, hissed and screamed as they leaped and scrambled and jumped off the roof. They made such a din that they set Sparks, the cocker spaniel, barking in the kitchen, and they set another dog barking, too. It was a long way off, but it barked dolefully, on and on. The long barking of the distant dog upset the owls. A little owl started his stark cry that wasn't unlike a bark. *Ah-uk*, *Ah-uk*, *Ah-uk*, went the little owl. *Whooo*! called a great tawny owl, as it scooped low over the roof and, seeing Galldora's eyes glint in the moonlight, dived and then flew away.

My eyes must be shining, thought Galldora. The owl turned, coming back for another look.

"Help! Hide me—I'm frightened of that owl," came a little voice, and Galldora saw the little cat, cringing against the chimney-stack. Galldora's motherly instincts were roused. She forgot how rude and conceited the little cat had been.

"Quick!" she called. "Come and hide with me—snuggle up, as close as you can, under my arm."

"Thank you," whimpered the little cat.

"Now, keep your head down," ordered Galldora, "and don't cry or make a move." The great owl came a third time over the chimney, and it alighted on the chimney-stack and stared down at Galldora.

"What in the world are you?" it asked.

"I'm a rag doll," answered Galldora, bravely.

"Fur," said the owl. "Fur—what's that fur?"

"Oh, that!" and Galldora laughed, gaily, "that's my fur coat, and I find it comfortable to lean against, you know."

"Really?" said the owl. "Really? And why are you on the roof, sitting up here so boldly? Don't you hide when you see me—or try to? I'm a great hunter, much feared."

"But why should I hide? I'm very unpleasant to eat," said Galldora, smiling brightly. "I'm so unpleasant to eat that even one bite at me would make you feel sick."

"Really?" said the owl, and blinked. "The things one learns," he said, and he flew off. As soon as the owl had gone, the little cat licked Galldora's face all over.

"Oh, thank you, thank you," he cried. "You're a real lady."

That's better, thought Galldora. "And are

you one of the gang now?" she asked. The little cat hung his head.

"Yes," he said, in a very low voice, "yes."

"Well, cheer up, then," said Galldora. "What are you so miserable about? You're a big cat now, and isn't that grand?"

"I suppose so," murmured the little cat, "only—only——"

"Only what?" asked Galldora.

"Only" —and the little cat looked at the rag doll with its wide eyes—"only, I can't get down. I did try, honestly I did. And when the big cats called out and told me to follow them, I pretended I was going the other way. But I hid, 'cause I didn't want to shame myself, and let them know that I couldn't get down, not after answering all those difficult questions—the ones you answered for me, I mean."

"That's a very sad story," said Galldora. "Well, I suppose you'll just have to stay up here."

"Yes," answered the little cat, "I'll have to stay until I grow big enough to climb down."

But the little cat wasn't very patient. As soon as a cock crowed the little cat said, "Oh, dear, I am thirsty." And when the robin woke, and sang loudly in the apple-tree below, the little cat said, "Oh, I would love some milk." And when the blackbird started up and woke the chaffinch, and he woke the wood-pigeons, and they woke a great many other birds, the little cat said, "I don't think I can wait until I grow up." And when Sparks, the spaniel, came rushing out of the back door and barked at the milkman in a friendly, tail-wagging way the little cat said, "I know I can't wait till I grow up," and he started to meow.

Once he had started to meow, the little cat went on meowing and meowing. Soon Sparks pricked up his ears and he sat on the lawn and looked up at the roof, then he barked. He could see the little cat walking round and round the chimney-stack, and in between his barks he could hear the little cat meowing. The barking brought out Marybell and Marybell's daddy. "What is it, old man?" asked Marybell's daddy.

"Look," Sparks barked, "look up there."

"Look, Daddy—look!" cried Marybell, who understood Sparks, "on the roof—it's a poor little pussy." Marybell's mummy joined them, then, and she looked up too. There they all stood and wondered what to do. But none of them saw Galldora. Galldora was very afraid nobody would notice her, so she said to the cat, "I've done you two good turns, haven't I?"

"Yes," said the little cat, "but I wish you could do me another and get me off this roof. I know I can't wait till I'm grown up."

"Oh, they'll get you down all right," said Galldora, "now that they've seen you, but do me a good turn, will you, and stand by me; then, when they come and get you, they'll notice me, too."

"All right," said the little cat, "you have been very kind to me, but oh! I must get down. I hate it here, I hate it here; I want some milk," and on and on cried the little cat, louder and louder.

Marybell's daddy fetched a ladder and, with

the help of two neighbours and the owner of the little cat, he climbed up to the roof and, just as he lifted the little cat, he saw the rag doll.

"Good gracious—Galldora—fancy finding you here." He picked Galldora up and brought her down, too.

He handed the little cat to the little cat's owner, who was delighted to have him back, and hurried him away to a big saucer of milk. Then he handed Galldora to Marybell, saying: "Of all your dolls, Marybell, Galldora is the strangest. Fancy getting on top of the roof!"

"I know," answered Marybell calmly. "Galldora is very strange, but she can't help it. I think it's because she's a rag doll."

The Heroine

ONE DAY THERE WAS A great squeaking and chattering among the toys in the nursery. It was not surprising, because Marybell had told them that next day her daddy was taking her to the sea, and they could all come too.

Now, one doll, Galldora, the rag doll, said nothing. She sat dreaming on the window-sill, dreaming of sea and sands. She did not expect that she would be taken. For, as Marybell had so often told her, "You are a disgrace to look at, Galldora."

Poor Galldora, her stuffing was weak, and her mouth was sewn on crookedly. But—well, Marybell never had the heart to throw her away, because she had been made by her favourite uncle, Uncle Jack.

Uncle Jack sailed on ships all over the world, and the ships took cargoes of bananas from here to there, and pineapples and dates, and china and glass, and other things as well. Uncle Jack was known as "Sparks" on his ship, and he was very important and knew all about sending out messages over the air. When Uncle Jack wasn't sending out messages or receiving messages, and when there wasn't a gale on, or a typhoon, or other sea troubles, Uncle Jack found time to make rugs and even to knit. But though Uncle Jack made ever so many rugs and knitted a great many socks, he only made one doll, and that was Galldora.

So Galldora was very special. Still, as she looked so queer, she was usually left sitting on the nursery window-sill when Marybell took the dolls and teddies on a special treat.

Next morning Marybell came into the nursery and collected up all her dolls and teddies, and the stuffed cat, Bobo, her spade, bucket, and the small shrimping-net. She put them in a pile in the middle of the floor, but she left Galldora where she was.

"Oh, but, Marybell, dear," said Marybell's mother, "you can't take all those. I said just one or two."

Marybell looked very sad. "But they all want to come," she said. Marybell was very understanding.

"Just take one doll and one teddy," said Marybell's mother firmly.

"But what about Bobo?" said Marybell.

"But cats don't like the sea, Marybell," said Marybell's mother.

"He would like the drive in the car," said Marybell, "and the teddies like being buried in the sand, and the French doll hasn't seen an English seaside, and Lulu likes sun-bathing, and so does Queenie, and Pansy wants to show off her new dress, and——"

"Really, dear," said Marybell's mother, "seven bears and ten dolls and a stuffed cat, are rather a lot."

"Couldn't they just sit in the car? I won't take them all out, really I won't," begged Marybell.

"Oh, very well," said Marybell's mother. Then she said: "But no more, mind you."

Marybell suddenly noticed Galldora on the window-sill. "Oh, but, Mummy," cried Marybell, "Galldora ought to come, oughtn't she? I mean, she's a real sailor doll, and she'd be so disappointed if she didn't go to the seaside. I know she would."

Marybell's mother sighed. "Well, perhaps Galldora wouldn't take up much room. But don't add any more."

"There aren't any others to take," said Marybell happily, as she started to collect up the dolls and teddies. She had to make four journeys down to the car, and then she had to come back to the nursery, as she had forgotten Galldora.

The big dolls sat on the picnic-basket on the back seat beside Marybell, and the bigger teddy bears were propped up by the side window with the towels and bathing things to sit on, and the smaller teddies and dolls were all arranged very comfortably on the ledge at the back window.

"I am very sorry," said Marybell's daddy, "but you will have to take some of those bears and things away from the back window, Marybell, because I can't see out."

So Marybell, with the help of her mother, rearranged the piles of teddies and dolls at the back. In the rearranging, Galldora got forgotten. She was left lying on the outside step by the back wheel.

The car started, and she went whizz out into the air but, luckily for Galldora, her hair had got jammed into the back door, which stopped her from being jerked right away. She had a most exciting ride.

It's just like flying, said Galldora to herself. And it was. She was quite airborne, except for

her wool hair. But at the corners, and every now and again, she went thud against the mudguard. I wouldn't be surprised, said Galldora to herself, if all these walloping bangs aren't the very best thing for my stuffing. After all, it will certainly get the dust out.

It was a good thing that Uncle Jack, though he was not very good at making rag dolls, had used strong sailcloth and thick twine to make Galldora. His stitches held very well, and Galldora was really none the worse for wear when they reached the seaside, except perhaps that her hair had grown a little with all the pulling.

"Oh, my poor Galldora!" cried Marybell, when she realized what had happened, and she gathered Galldora up in her arms and took her straight away on to the sands. Galldora was sat up against the picnic-basket. She gazed out at the blue, blue sea, and the silver-gold sands, and at the sky touching the far waves, and at the white seagulls going flap, flap, flap up and down the beach.

"My!" said Galldora happily, "this does bring back memories." Her shoe-button eyes shone, and she hummed a sea-chanty she remembered. She hummed very, very softly, so that no one could hear; and her sea-chanty, which had a very delightful tune, got all muddled up in the rumbing noise of the waves as they rolled the sand and the shells out, and then rolled them back again.

It was a wonderful morning, really one of the most wonderful mornings in Galldora's life. When she wasn't humming sea-chanties she watched all seven teddy bears being buried in the sand, and she waved, when no one was looking, at the stuffed cat, who sat proudly on the top of a sand castle. The big dolls, and the new French one, Allouette, had been left in the car to sun-

bathe through the window, while some of the other dolls had been dipped in the sea and taught swimming.

Nothing, thought Galldora, can go wrong with to-day. But she was mistaken. In the afternoon Marybell's daddy took Marybell for a sail, far out on the waves, in his rubber dinghy.

Marybell had insisted that Bobo and Galldora wanted to come. She was quite wrong, because Bobo didn't want to go—he really did hate water, it made him have a funny feeling in his whiskers.

They sailed far, far out to sea. Then, oh, dear!

A dreadful thing happened. The rubber dinghy got a puncture. It must have hit a sharp rock or a sunken piece of iron, or a wreck, or something. Marybell started to cry, and Marybell's daddy, who knew all about rubber dinghies and leaks, looked very worried. Marybell's mother and the picnic-basket seemed very, very far away.

Marybell knew Bobo would be the most frightened, and so she kept on saying "It's all right, Bobo, it's all right."

Marybell's daddy said nothing. He looked very grim. The water kept sloshing in, and everything got wet. Then Marybell's daddy thought of a good idea.

"Hand me the rag doll," he said calmly. He pinched and squeezed Galldora into the leaking hole. Her head was stuck right down into the sea. "There," said Marybell's father cheerfully, "that ought to get us safely back. Hang on to her legs, Marybell." Marybell did.

Dear me, thought Galldora to herself, this is most extraordinary. There's no wind down here and no sound, and I do wish the jelly-fish would mind where they are going.

It wasn't very long before her head got muddled up with the pebbles and the shells that the surf was rolling backward and forward.

One of her eyes got torn right away, and suddenly one arm got caught upon a great nail in the breakwater.

"Help!" cried Galldora. "Help!" But no one heard. She seemed to be tugged in all directions. Marybell was tugging at her legs, and her arm was being torn off in the other direction. Uncle Jack's stitches were strained to their utmost.

"Oh, dear! Oh, help!" cried Galldora. "This is dreadful." Then the rubber boat gave an extra heave, and they were on the sands.

When they pulled Galldora up she had only one eye, very little hair, and no dress left to speak of, and she was so flabby and wet that Marybell burst into tears.

Marybell's daddy picked up Galldora and rung her out. "She's a heroine," he said. "She's a brave doll. She's saved us all."

Then he grinned, for the rag doll really did look very funny, but Galldora gasped. A heroine, she said to herself, so that's what I am, a real heroine.

Galldora was taken back to Marybell's mummy and the picnic-basket, and the whole adventure was told.

"Poor, brave Galldora," said Marybell's mummy. "I will certainly have to sew on a new eye and make Galldora a new dress. We can't have heroines in rags."

"She'd better have a medal too, for lifesaving," said Marybell's daddy.

"Well, I never!" Galldora was amazed. "They really do seem to think a lot of me."

Galldora was given the very best place on the back window of the car as she rode home in great style. The dolls and teddies treated her with respect and admiration. "I wouldn't be surprised if you were knighted," said the Big Teddy in his gruff, kind voice. "Then you would have a 'Sir' before your name."

Sir Galldora, thought Galldora to herself. Yes, that would sound very nice.

"I'm very glad it wasn't me that had to fill the hole," said Bobo humbly, in his tiny, dry voice. "And I think you are terribly brave, Galldora."

Galldora smiled, she hardly heard, she was dreaming away to herself. "Sir Galldora," she kept on repeating softly. "Yes, I like that very much—Sir Galldora." And she gazed out on the passing world, with her one shining eye. "Sir Galldora, the great heroine—that's me, an important, lifesaving rag doll." And she practised bowing to the passing trees and the cows, as if they were cheering crowds.

Galldora and the Woods-beyond

THERE WAS ONE TREAT that the dolls and teddy bears and the stuffed cat Bobo loved almost more than any other treat. And that was to be taken to the woods-beyond. One or two, or sometimes even three of them, were taken there when Marybell went to pick bluebells in the spring or coloured leaves in the autumn.

Now, poor Galldora was the only doll that had never been to the woods-beyond. She always pretended she didn't mind. "Oh, woods," Galldora would say, "they are unkept, wild places. I much prefer gardens, where there is grass and flowers and paths all in order."

"But you should see the woods, Galldora," Bobo, the stuffed cat, once said. "When the bluebells are out, Galldora, the woods look like a lake, it really does. A shining lake of blue, with the trees looking as if they were growing in the water."

"And the birds singing," growled the Teddy Bear softly, "I thought it was fairies singing at first, till Marybell said they were birds."

"Birds," said Galldora, in a very high, trying-not-to-cry voice, "I prefer a blackbird's song to any others. You should have heard the blackbird sing from the garden-shed this afternoon, but of course you were out."

Then Galldora pressed her head closer to the nursery window, she did not want the Big Teddy to see that her shoe-button eyes were full of unspilt tears.

The woods-beyond, if only I could see them once, thought Galldora.

One spring night, after the dolls and teddy bears had talked even more about the woods-beyond, Galldora felt so sad she could not sleep. "I don't care," she kept on saying, but she did. She stayed awake and just stared out into the cool silvery garden. She stared and stared, and all the black polish on her eyes grew dim. She bumped her head so many times against the window-pane that her wool plaits frayed out and became all unplaited. Her face grew even whiter, and her sewn-on mouth seemed to turn down a little.

Next day Marybell said, "Dolls and teddy bears, I've got a wonderful treat for you. My daddy is taking us in a car, and we are going for a picnic. Won't that be fun, my darlings?"

I wonder if she will take me too, said Galldora to herself.

Marybell put all the dolls and teddies on the floor. Then she collected them in armfuls and took them to the car. Galldora was in the last armful to be carried out and she fell, unnoticed, to the floor.

Galldora lay for some time on the nursery floor, staring at the ceiling. She heard the gay chatter and laughter in the hall as the picnic party collected. She heard Marybell's daddy starting up the car in the garage. She heard the car back round to the front door. She heard them all climb in, and then she heard the car door slam. She heard the car start on its way. She heard it hoot at the end of the drive. She heard the car purr into the distance, and for a long time after that she continued lying on the floor, staring at the ceiling.

"I don't think I can bear to hear them all talking of the picnic. They'll tell me all about it, every bit of it, and it will make me more and more sad."

Suddenly the nursery door was pushed slowly open. Galldora stayed very still. Sparks, the spaniel dog, came and sniffed her. Galldora kept very silent. Then Sparks patted her with his paw. Galldora was so flabby that when the dog patted her she jumped, and this amused Sparks. He wagged his tail. He patted her again. Galldora leaped into the air, and fell with a soft *plop*. Then Sparks closed his teeth very softly and gently round Galldora, and he ran with her from the room, wagging his tail delightedly.

He trotted down the stairs with Galldora in his mouth. He went into the garden and put Galldora down on the lawn. He looked at her. Then he pushed her around with his nose again and patted her up into the air with his paws.

The cook flung open the kitchen window and shouted, "What have you got there, Sparks? Put it down at once, you naughty dog."

Sparks looked round in a guilty way. He quickly picked Galldora up again, with a gentle mouth, for he was really a good dog, and ran out of the garden, into the field, and on to the woods.

Once in the woods, Sparks put Galldora down very gently on to a bed of moss against a tree. Sparks sniffed the sweet air. Rabbits, he sniffed.

He was soon barking joyfully at the rabbit-holes. Then running and jumping at the rustles in the tangles of briar and weeds, here, then there, then farther on. Galldora looked about her. "The wood—this must be the woods-beyond." There was magic in the very thought. All about the wood was a strange light, a blue sheen of light.

At first Galldora could not think where the light came from. Then she noticed it came as if from the bluebells, which were flowering and moving gently in the breeze, like waves on a shining sheet of blue water. Near her was a clump of late primroses. Butterflies flittered in twos and threes, joyfully, looking like flowers as they fluttered. The branches made a canopy of pale green, and the pussy-willow and the last of the catkins were like signposts to the sunshine.

Over all, and above the chatter of the rooks, came the ringing, bell-like call of a great tit and the flute of a robin and the softly trickling song of the willow warbler.

The birds singing in the woods-beyond, I have heard them, I have heard them, said Galldora to herself, and gave a long, happy sigh.

After seeking rabbits and finding none Sparks went home and forgot about the rag doll. But Galldora didn't even notice, she was so happy.

The rain came and pattered down on to Galldora's woolly head. The moon came out and glinted on Galldora's black shoe-button eyes. Then the dawn broke and set a soft glow stealing over Galldora's white rag face. All the time Galldora kept saying: "I am in the woods-beyond, I am in the woods-beyond." After two nights and two days Galldora was still in a dream of happiness, sitting on her soft cushion of moss, propped against the tree, with the robins chirping about her and the butterflies sometimes resting on her rag hand.

None of the other dolls and none of the teddies, or even Bobo, the stuffed cat, have been in the wood at night, thought Galldora. But I have.

After three days Marybell came up to the woods to pick bluebells, and she brought Sparks. Sparks suddenly remembered Galldora. He

dashed here and there and sniffed her out. He took her up and worried her, growling in a friendly way.

"Sparks—here—good dog!" called Marybell. "Here, Sparks, what have you found?" Sparks bounded up to his mistress with Galldora hanging limply from his mouth "Why!" gasped Marybell, "it's my very own rag doll!" She gazed at Galldora in a motherly way and shook her head sadly. "Poor old thing," she said, "poor old, silly old thing, you are in a mess. Wet through and so dirty. I'll have to dry you out by the fire, and sew a new dress on you. Come on, let's get you home at once, or you'll catch a dreadful cold." Galldora was carried home and seated in the best place against the nursery fender.

"We've been for three picnics now, Galldora," said Bobo. Galldora smiled.

"Up on the downs. Oh, you should see the downs, Galldora," growled the Big Teddy. "They are my favourite place." Galldora just smiled.

"Oh, you should go in a car some time, Galldora," said Lulu. Galldora hardly listened. She was so happy, and still dreaming of the magic of the woods-beyond.

"What a pity you haven't seen the stream where we picnic, but perhaps next time," said Little White Teddy Bear to Galldora, as kindly as he could.

"The woods-beyond," sighed Galldora in a dreamy way.

"Magic," said Galldora, still in a dream. "At night," said Galldora, hardly above a whisper. "At night."

The teddy bears were silent, and the dolls

looked at each other. Then Galldora told them all about it.

"How brave you are, Galldora," said Bobo, "to have been in the woods-beyond at night all by yourself."

"Oh! the moonlight and the owls," murmured Galldora. "It's magic! Oh, yes! It's the best place of all—the woods-beyond at night."

Galldora and the Rabbit Pie

"I DO SO WANT A RABBIT," said Marybell. The rabbit she wanted was a small black and white one, and the rabbit was owned by a boy called Tony. "Oh, please," begged Marybell, holding the rabbit very tightly, "please, Tony, won't you give him to me?"

"No," said Tony firmly, "and you're squeezing it, Marybell. Give him back." Marybell handed back the small rabbit.

The rabbit's mother was peeping out of the open door of her hutch, very anxiously. She knew one of her eight babies was out and she waffled her nose and pricked her ears. Tony put the baby rabbit back, closed the hutch, and went on cleaning up the yard. He took no more notice of Marybell. Marybell, very sadly, went out of Tony's garden. She stopped for just a brief moment at the gate and looked at the notice again. She couldn't read very well, but she knew it said:

LOTS OF RABBITS FOR SALE. TWO AND SIXPENCE EACH. APPLY TONY ACKROYD, THE WILLOWS, QUEXON HILL, MERRYFIELDS. TELEPHONE NUMBER, MERRYFIELDS 246.

"I think he's a jolly mean, stinky little boy," said Marybell furiously, after she had looked at the notice, and she went home, walking in her special strutty way that made her plaid skirt swirl.

"Can I have two shillings and sixpence?" Marybell asked her Mummy at lunch.

"Certainly not!" answered Marybell's mother.

"Money's getting very expensive," said Marybell, "and three pennies a week doesn't last out."

"It's quite enough for a little girl," answered Marybell's mother firmly.

When Marybell's daddy came back from work Marybell said, "Please, Daddy, can I have two shillings and sixpence?"

"Now, you know, Marybell," said Marybell's daddy, "we said three pennies a week and no more, didn't we?"

"But I want it for something very special," said Marybell seriously. Marybell's daddy was not in a very talkative mood. He wasn't really listening to Marybell; he was thinking of other things.

"I can't tell you what it is," went on Marybell, "for it's a secret, but I want it for a very, very, very special reason."

"Isn't it your bedtime yet?" said Marybell's father. Marybell gave a big sigh. It was clearly going to be no good asking her daddy for two shillings and sixpence.

When Marybell was in bed, and before she went to sleep she had a long, deep think about the two and sixpence and the rabbit. It was such a dear little thing, so small and furry, and so very soft. It had such very black ears and such very black paws and such queer black dots and dashes down its back. Its eyes were blue, not red, which Marybell thought was much more attractive. Some of the other babies had brown markings and some were almost quite white. Some had pointed faces, but this one—the one that Marybell really wanted—had a broad, flat face. "It's got to be mine," said Marybell before she went to sleep. "It's simply got to be mine."

When Marybell woke up it was very early. She always woke up very early, and there was a long, long wait before Marybell's mummy and daddy got up. Marybell at once thought about the rabbit. She dressed herself, and went out of the house and down the road. She went to Quexon

Hill and into Tony's garden. She opened the rabbit-hutch and looked at the babies. She put her hand into the bundle of babies and found the black-nosed rabbit, and took it out and cuddled it.

"Hi," called a voice, "put that rabbit back!" Marybell looked round. There was Tony standing watching her.

"I want it," said Marybell.

"Where's your two and six?" said Tony, quite unmoved. Marybell was a little frightened of

Tony. Tony was a whole four years older than Marybell.

"I haven't got two and six," said Marybell, putting on her baby voice, "but I want the baby rabbit, please, Tony."

"Well, you can't have it," answered Tony. "Put it back at once." If Tony had been a grown-up Marybell's baby voice would have had results. It nearly always did, but Tony wasn't grown-up, and Tony was quite unmoved. He stood there in his khaki shorts and striped jersey, with his hair very much on end, hands in his pockets, and just stared. Marybell knew she had to do as he said. So she put the rabbit back. She closed the door of the hutch. She stood sucking her thumb. "Go home," ordered Tony, "your mother will be missing you."

"She isn't up yet," said Marybell. It was a lovely morning, cool and sunny, with the promise of great heat later on. The bees were thick in the catmint and the lavender. The roses, washed with the night dew, looked shining and clear. The white pigeons were cooing on the dovecote, and a young blackbird was pecking at a strawberry through the net in the silent kitchen garden.

"Why can't I have the baby rabbit?" asked Marybell, pouting.

"Because you haven't got two and six," said Tony, keeping his eyes very round and unblinking.

"I'll give you a sucky sweet," said Marybell hopefully.

"I don't want one," said Tony.

"I'll get three pennies for my pocket money tomorrow," said Marybell. "You can have that."

"Three pennies are not enough," answered Tony, still standing very solidly and squarely in the path.

"Well, I've got seven farthings saved up," went on Marybell.

"That's only a penny and three farthings," said Tony.

"But I can't get two whole shillings," said Marybell drooping her lip.

"Two shillings and sixpence," corrected Tony.

"I can't get it, I tell you," said Marybell. "Mummy won't give it to me, and my daddy won't give it to me."

"Well, then, you can't have the rabbit," answered Tony.

"But how do you get money?" asked Marybell, almost in tears. She did so want the rabbit.

"You have to work to get money," said Tony. "I clean out my rabbits, and go out and collect dandelions and grass, and I have to go to the farm and ask for the straw and collect it. There's a lot of work in keeping rabbits. Why don't you go home and work?" Marybell's eyes began to swim with tears.

"I'm a very little girl," she said.

"You're not as little as my baby sister," said Tony. "How old are you?"

"I'm not going to tell you," answered Marybell crossly.

"My baby sister is two," said Tony. There didn't seem to be any answer to that, so Marybell went back to her home and her breakfast very sadly.

Nobody seemed to notice that Marybell was a very sad girl. Everybody in the house was extra busy. They were busy because a visitor was coming to dinner. The visitor was a captain. The captain was so important that there was extra cleaning and dusting and cooking to be done. There were flowers to be arranged and, oh, all sorts of things to be done, and nobody was at all interested in Marybell.

She went up to her nursery and looked at all her dolls and didn't want to play with any of them. She looked at her teddies, and they all seemed very dull compared to the baby rabbit. She went to the nursery window, and on the window-sill was her old rag doll, Galldora. Inside Galldora were the seven farthings. They were kept there for safe-keeping. Marybell took up Galldora and went back to Tony. She found Tony in a garden-shed, playing with his train.

"I've brought you my rag doll," said Marybell.

"What for?" asked Tony.

"She's got seven farthings sewn up inside her," said Marybell. "I keep them there for safe-keeping. You can have Galldora and the farthings if I can have the rabbit."

"But I don't like dolls," said Tony, without looking up. "I like trains and soldiers. Haven't you got any soldiers?"

"No," said Marybell, "but Galldora's a very nice rag doll, though she is a bit flabby now. She's as old as I am." Tony looked at Galldora. He took her and examined her. She had shoe-button eyes. Well, he thought, the shoe buttons might come in useful. She had wool hair, but the wool was too weak for tying up anything; and she had a dress which could be cut off and might come in useful for polishing his trains, but it wasn't a very long dress.

"She's not worth much," said Tony, handing her back.

"Would you like one of my teddies?" asked Marybell hopefully.

"I've got my own teddy, and I don't want another," said Tony. "And I think dolls are silly things. The only fun you can have with dolls is cutting off their hair. Haven't you got a train?" Marybell shook her head. "Oh, well," said Tony, "you'll have to get two shillings and sixpence."

"Can I go and just hold the baby rabbit for a little while, please?" begged Marybell.

"No," said Tony, "you'll only upset the mother." Marybell started to cry. Tony watched her. He was very much alarmed. He didn't like girls crying and he always got into trouble when his baby sister cried. "I'll tell you what," he said, "you can have the rabbit for a shilling."

"Oh, can I really?" said Marybell, cheering up.

"Yes," said Tony, "that's letting you off a whole shilling and sixpence, and it means I can't get as many soldiers as I'd planned to. Still, you can have the rabbit for a shilling."

After the first moment of joy Marybell was suddenly downcast again. "But where am I to get a shilling from?" she asked.

"Go home and help your mummy," said Tony, "and she'll give you a shilling." Marybell went happily home. She was quite certain that Tony knew about everything and all she had to do now was to help her mummy.

The hours were passing and still nothing was ready for the visit of the captain. Marybell's mother was to-ing and fro-ing from room to room.

"Can I help you, mummy?" asked Marybell.

"No, dear, not now," answered Marybell's mother absent-mindedly, and went on talking out loud, but really to herself, "Oh, dear! We really do need another vase of flowers over in that corner. It does look very dull without them, and the captain is a great gardener, so I think roses. Robert, dear, could I pick some more roses?"

Marybell's daddy, in rolled-up shirt sleeves and with a worried frown on his face, said "Oh, Mary! Do you really have to have any more roses? There won't be any left in the garden, and the captain is an expert on roses and I did so want——"

"All right, Robert, I'll get some syringa."

"Daddy," asked Marybell, following her daddy into the garden, "can I help you?"

"No, Marybell, not to-day. Now, where did I put the spanner. I'll never get the lawn cut in time. Well? What is it, Marybell?"

"I want to help you, Daddy."

"Look, Marybell, dear, just run away and play, can't you? There's a good girl."

Marybell stood on the lawn, holding Galldora by the leg and swinging her up and down. Marybell was thinking deeply. Then she went into the kitchen. On the kitchen-table was a milk bottle, a rolling-pin, and some pastry left on a marble slab, for Marybell's mother was wonderful at making puff pastry. There was an earthenware dish with some cooked rabbit and gravy. Marybell propped Galldora up against the milk bottle and stood staring at the table, thinking. She wondered if she dare roll out the pastry. Would her mother be pleased, or very cross? She decided her mother would be very cross. The kitchen was cool and neat, and all the washing up had been done. In the basket was Sparks, the spaniel, and everything was in order.

Perhaps I could help by making tea, thought Marybell. So she lifted down the electric kettle and filled it with water from the tap at the sink by standing on a chair. It was rather heavy and, struggling back with it, she knocked the table. The pie-dish started to wobble. Marybell's mother had left it far too near the edge. It wobbled for a long time while Marybell stood

still, watching it. She had the kettle in her hand and couldn't think how to manage the kettle and stop the dish wobbling.

Sparks too was greatly interested in the wobbling dish. He watched it with his spaniel ears pricked as far as a spaniel's ears could be pricked. Then, with a *splosh*, the dish fell onto the linoleum floor. Sparks was now very interested. While Marybell put the kettle on to the table near the cooker Sparks had left his basket and gobbled and gobbled up most of the rabbit.

"Naughty Sparks!" scolded Marybell. She put back the two small bits of rabbit that were left and as much of the vegetables as she could scoop up with a spoon, and as much of the gravy as she could, then she mopped up the rest with the dish-cloth and squeezed it into the pie. She was thankful the dish hadn't broken. But Marybell was worried. The dish did look very empty now, and if her mummy knew what had happened she would never get her shilling.

Then Marybell's eyes fell on Galldora. She picked Galldora up and pushed her into the pie-dish. The pie-dish looked almost full, with Galldora squeezed down and the two bits of rabbit, the vegetables, and the gravy on top.

Help! thought Galldora. Help!

Just then Marybell's mother came into the kitchen and, as she was in a terrible fluster because the captain had arrived an hour earlier than he was expected, she didn't look closely at the pie. She rolled out the pastry and popped it on to the top of Galldora and the gravy.

Oh, dear me! thought Galldora. Now what?

Galldora didn't have to wonder long, for she was lifted up in the pie-dish and put into a hot oven.

This is terrible, said Galldora to herself. This is terrible. I don't like this a bit. It's all dark and stuffy, and the gravy is all getting into my hair.

The pie-dish grew hotter and hotter, and Galldora grew more and more nervous.

I am sure I shall just disappear, she kept thinking, and then there won't be any ME left.

Marybell's mother, having put the pie into the oven, had dashed upstairs to change her dress and brush her hair. Marybell's daddy had taken the captain into the garden to show him the roses.

Marybell was left standing in the kitchen, nervously wondering if her rag doll was all right. She felt very sorry for Galldora and hadn't realized, not really, that Galldora would have to go into the oven. Marybell was so upset that she got into Sparks' basket and cuddled up with him.

Marybell's mother came into the kitchen, saw Marybell, and said: "Oh, Marybell, really! You are being most irritating to-day. Just look at you! All covered with dog's hairs."

Marybell was dragged upstairs, scrubbed and and washed, and her hair brushed and brushed, and she was put into her best blue dress, with blue ribbons in her hair; and her socks were changed for her very best white socks, and her shoes for her best white sandals. Then she was taken down to the drawing-room.

"Aha," said the captain, "so here's the little girl."

"Do you like rabbits?" asked Marybell at once, hoping that the captain might say Yes and buy her the baby rabbit from Tony.

"The captain simply loves rabbit, don't you, Captain?" said Marybell's daddy.

"What, what?" said the captain, puffing a little through his very fine and well-trimmed moustache.

"My wife always remembers that you love rabbit pie, don't you, Mary?"

Marybell's mother smiled and said, "Yes, I always remember."

The captain spluttered a little. "Excellent, excellent!" he said at last. Marybell, watching, didn't miss a single expression on the captain's face.

"You know, Marybell," explained Marybell's daddy, "the first time the captain came to lunch, your mother gave him one of her rabbit pies, and he said rabbit pie was his favourite meal."

"Did he?" said Marybell. But she wasn't at all sure that he did, because, for just a second, the captain had that sort of face on, that she herself put on, when she had to eat cornflour pudding, which she simply hated.

At last lunch was ready. After the soup in came the rabbit pie. Marybell was feeling very nervous and fidgety. She wondered what they'd say about Galldora.

"I think it's awfully cruel to eat rabbits," she said. No one took any notice of her remark, and Marybell's daddy cut the puff pastry and then tried to get out a piece of rabbit. He found it very difficult. Marybell was feeling very, very nervous. "I think it's awfully cruel to eat rabbits," she said louder. Marybell's mother was looking anxious and the captain was pretending not to notice, and Marybell's daddy was having a very difficult time indeed. At last he got the fork all twisted up in Galldora's hair and, with a *plop*, out came Galldora's head. Marybell's mother screamed, and Marybell's daddy gasped, "What on earth...?" He was staring down at two shoe-button eyes. "I think it's awfully cruel to eat rabbits," said Marybell, as loudly as she could.

"Why, it's Galldora!" said Marybell's daddy, as he pulled out a long, weak-looking rag doll.

"Marybell! Oh, you bad girl!" sobbed Marybell's mother.

"I think it's awfully cruel to eat rabbits," said

Marybell stubbornly. The captain burst into laughter.

"Quite right, my dear, quite right. You stick to your idea. You thought it was cruel to eat rabbit, so you gave us your doll to eat instead. Was that it?"

Marybell, at last finding somebody listening to her, said very quickly and all at once, "I was helping because I wanted a shilling to buy one of Tony's baby rabbits—the black and white one. Oh, it's ever so sweet. He's got eight and he said I could have one for a shilling, and he said my mummy would give me a shilling if I helped her, so I did try to help, but it all went wrong. Oh, it is such a sweet baby rabbit!"

The captain gave Marybell a shilling and said, "There, that's for the baby rabbit." He seemed in very good spirits and said he enjoyed eating just potatoes and butter; he liked nothing better.

After lunch the captain decided to go with Marybell to get the rabbit. He told Marybell as they walked down the road together that he was delighted that Galldora was in the pie, for if there was one thing he really hated eating it was rabbit pie; but he asked Marybell to keep it a great secret, as he didn't want to hurt her mummy's

feelings. Marybell quite understood, and was very pleased to keep the secret.

And Galldora—well, after a good wash, Galldora was pegged on to the line and left to dry. She really didn't look any the worse for her rough treatment. She hung there, proudly telling all the bees and butterflies that flew about her, "I saved the whole situation by being baked in a pie."

Galldora and the Mermaid

ONE DAY GALLDORA was given a new dress and taken by Marybell to the seaside for a holiday.

"What a strange doll," said the landlady, Mrs Cockle, when she saw Galldora.

"She's not really strange," answered Marybell, "she's just a rag doll." Marybell spoke as stiffly as she could, because she was upset that the landlady was so rude about Galldora.

"Yes, my dear, I can see she is a rag doll," said the landlady slowly, "but she's strange all the same. She's very faded and flabby, poor thing, but perhaps the sea air will do her good. Let's hope so."

"It's just her new dress that makes her look washed out," explained Marybell, talking very fast to get in all she wanted to say. "It is rather a bright colour. It's a piece of Mummy's worn-out dance dress. Mummy calls it flame colour. I'm

not sure I like that colour myself. Blue's my favourite colour, that's why I bought a blue ribbon for Galldora's hair. I spent a whole fourpence on that ribbon. The colour's called kingfisher blue, and it doesn't look quite right with flame colour, but it is pretty all the same."

"Very pretty," Mrs Cockle said, adding, "It's a pity about the safety-pin though, it's so large that it hides most of the ribbon."

"Well, but, you see, Mrs Cockle, I had to pin it on Galldora's hair, because Galldora can't keep ribbons on her hair. It's wool hair, Mrs Cockle, and it's got a bit moth-eaten, and her head's such a funny shape too, sort of flattish, do you see what I mean?"

Galldora was held up for inspection. Mrs Cockle inspected Galldora's head. "Yes, very flat, my dear, and a very odd shape."

Now, Galldora was not at all pleased at this conversation. She loved being looked at, but she felt it was very rude indeed of people to make remarks on the shape of her head.

Human beings, she thought to herself, have no manners, no manners at all. Certainly none where dolls are concerned.

I think the discussion on Galldora's head would have spoilt the whole of Galldora's holiday if it hadn't been for an adventure that came her way on the first evening.

It was a wonderful adventure, and Galldora was able to tell all the other dolls and the teddy bears about it when she returned to the nursery. It happened like this. Marybell was so eager to rush down to the sands and the sea at once that her mother promised to take her down as soon as they had unpacked the spade, the bucket, and the swimsuits.

"We won't wait for lunch," said Marybell's mother, "we'll ask Mrs Cockle if she could make us some sandwiches and we'll eat them on the sands."

Mrs Cockle understood all about little girls wanting to rush on to the sands and not waste a moment, so she bustled about and produced a packed lunch.

"There you are, my dear," she said to Marybell's mother, as she handed over the lunch, and turning to Marybell she added, "That's right, love, you take that doll down and give her a good sea blow, that will do the poor thing a power of good."

The sands and the sea were all that sands and sea should be. The sands were silver white, stretching as far to the right and as far to the left as Marybell could see, and the great ocean was in a very gentle mood.

"Oh, Mummy," said Marybell, "I want to stay here always and always."

"Well, we have till six o'clock," answered Marybell's mother. "Now, how about a paddle, Marybell, while I get the lunch set out? Then after lunch I'll help you build a sand castle, and later we will go and have a real swim."

So after their lunch Marybell's mother helped Marybell to build the hugest and the most magnificent sand castle that Galldora had ever seen. It was so large that Marybell could stand in the middle courtyard without knocking any of the castle walls down. The castle had turrets and windows, and a moat, and a wall round the moat, with more turrets and more windows. When the castle was finished Galldora was sat on a sand-throne made specially for her. She sat there happily and proudly staring out over the castle walls.

After a swim Marybell decided to look for shells. She and her mother were so happy collecting shells and shining wet pebbles that Marybell's mother forgot all about the time. When she did look at her watch she was horrified.

"Quickly, Marybell," she said, "we mustn't be late the very first day. Mrs Cockle said she would have a high tea waiting for us at six, and it is six o'clock now."

There was a lot of collecting-up to be done. Wet towels and bathing-suits were crammed into one basket. Then into another basket went the paper wrappings of the lunch and the sun-hats and the sun-glasses, while in the bucket went the pebbles and shells. With all the pushing of this here and that there, both Marybell and Marybell's mother forgot Galldora. Marybell's mother did say, "Have you got Galldora, Marybell?" and

Marybell had answered, "Yes, Mummy, I put her with my swim-suit." And Marybell really thought she had. Galldora couldn't be seen, for the sand-throne she had been sitting on had collapsed, and she had sunk forward against the wall. She was still upright, and her head rested against a turret, but she was hidden and she couldn't see anything but sand. Galldora heard Marybell chattering as she and her mother hurried away from the beach, back to Mrs Cockle and high tea. Soon the beach grew very quiet except for the wild noises of sea-birds. Then the noise of the sea seemed to grow louder.

The half-hours went by, and the sky changed from blue to a flush of pink and yellow gold. If only Galldora could have seen how wonderful the sky was, for it looked just as if some giant child of the sky-lands had tipped up a basket full of rose petals and set them floating down. Then the colour left the sky, and a silver bloom lingered on all the sea and the sands. All the while the sound of the sea grew louder.

I know I'm not fancying it, said Galldora to herself. It's true, the sea is coming towards me inch by inch.

It was true. The tide was rolling in the white surf, and with the incoming tide a low wind had sprung up. The wind stirred the white sand and set the white horses riding far out at sea. It may have been the dragging of the sands, as the sea washed out before each incoming wave swept up, or it may have been the low wind shifting the sands, but whatever was the cause, the walls of the castle cracked and slowly, very slowly, crumbled.

"Gracious me," gasped Galldora, "I can see now—and how very different everything looks. Mrs Cockle wouldn't approve at all. Why everything looks as pale and as washed-out as my face."

The silver bloom about the scene turned clearer and harder. Shadows sprung like seaweed in a silver wash. All in the dark and the light of the waves were a million phosphorous sea life, that glowed so gaily it looked as if the fish were holding a great ball, far down below. The moon, like a full-sailed ship riding high, seemed to let drift a fishing-net of light to glitter and shimmer on the sea.

It's very beautiful, thought Galldora, but I rather wish I wasn't here. I think Mrs Cockle's boarding-house would be more cosy. Still, it's no good me wishing, as here I am and here I'll have to stay until Marybell finds me to-morrow.

All the time the sea crept closer, wave by wave. This began to worry Galldora.

I wish the sea would stop—just stop where it is, thought Galldora. If it doesn't my castle will soon be washed away and I with it. And then she sighed, "Oh, dear, poor Marybell, she won't have a rag doll any more."

Just then Galldora thought she heard sweet singing. I've got myself into such a state of nerves, I'm imagining all sorts of things, she told herself crossly. Why, that's only the noise of the sea or the wind or a bird. But try as Galldora would to make herself believe the singing noise was just natural noises, she couldn't. The singing grew louder and higher. I don't think I like that singing at all, thought Galldora, it makes me feel uncomfortable.

Then Galldora noticed a shape on one of the white horses far out in the sea. As the shape came nearer Galldora thought it was a girl. A girl with long, shining hair. And it was a girl. The girl was singing.

Nearer and nearer came the white horse and the girl with the long hair, until with a sudden *splosh*, she was washed up on shore. Then Galldora saw she was not a proper girl, but a mermaid.

The mermaid was in a shocking temper. She clearly hated being on the shore. She stopped singing and lashed her tail, and was very thankful when the next wave lifted her up and washed her out into the sea again.

"Oh, do stop and talk to me, please?" called Galldora. "I've never talked to a mermaid before. But perhaps you can't talk."

"Of course I can, silly," answered the mermaid. "But where are you?"

"In here," called Galldora, "here in the sand castle." The mermaid swam close to the shore to have a look.

"I can't see with all this hair," said the mermaid at last, and she tossed her hair this way and that.

"I'm just near you," explained Galldora, "for the sea has come up to my castle walls, and I'm terribly afraid it will wash it and me away."

The mermaid lifted up her silvery hair with her two hands. "That's better," she said. "Ah, yes, I can see you now. My, aren't you small, and you haven't got much hair—how very strange."

"Oh, yes, I know all about that," said poor Galldora. "And I've got a funny shaped head, but I'm used to it, and it's *my* hair and *my* head, and, anyway, talking of hair, you've got far too much. You ought to have it cut off."

"Cut it off—how do you do that?" asked the mermaid. Then Galldora realized at once she had made a very silly remark, because, of course, who would have scissors in the sea. "Oh, I've changed my mind," she said hurriedly, "I shouldn't cut your hair off if I were you; it suits you."

"If you had to choose between one eye and three eyes," said the mermaid, "which would you choose?"

"I've often had one eye," said Galldora, "and

another one can always be sewn on, but three would look ugly, very ugly indeed. So I would choose one."

"I'd choose three," said the mermaid, "a third one in the middle of my forehead, then when I opened my middle eye, the lashes would lift my hair a little, so I could see. It's a dreadful nuisance not being able to see properly. Look what happened just now. I got washed ashore, just because I couldn't see where I was going."

"Yes, I do understand what you mean," said Galldora thoughtfully.

"Can't you think of something to help me?" asked the mermaid.

"I'll try," said Galldora. "You can see now, though, can't you?"

"Yes, because I'm lifting my hair with my hands, but it gets trying."

"Of course," said Galldora. Then she asked, "Do other mermaids have this trouble?"

"No," answered the mermaid. "It's because I'm a bad mermaid I have this trouble. The good mermaids sit on rocks and sing to the sailors, and it makes the sailors muddled and then they wreck their ships on the rocks. The ships sink, and the mermaids go swimming down and down into the wrecks and they find all sorts of

treasures, like string and mirrors and combs. The mermaids make their hair behave by combing it, then they tie it up with the string, and then they look at themselves in the mirrors."

"Just a moment," said Galldora. "I'm getting a bit muddled, or are you? Surely if mermaids wreck ships that's being very wicked and bad."

"No, that's being good," said the mermaid. "Being bad is being like me, not wrecking ships, but just playing about in the sea. Oh, I love playing!"

"I think I'll have to think this out," muttered Galldora, feeling very muddled.

Just then a crab who had been silently listening started to laugh and said, "what a joke —thinking."

"It's all very well for you to laugh," said Galldora crossly, "but you don't have to think this out like I do. You understand the sea and sea-creatures. I don't."

"Don't try," answered the crab. "Some folks do things sideways, like me, some folks do things flat ways, like plaice, while other folks do things along, like eels do. But mermaids, they do things upside down."

"Yes. "Galldora had a long think. "That's very helpful," she said." Thank you, Mr Crab, for telling me. I understand now. Being good is being bad to mermaids and being bad is being good, is that it?"

"It is and it isn't," answered the crab, "it just depends. Now, for instance, mermaids take a lot of trouble to save sailors' lives, after wrecking their ships. You can't reason with mermaids, it's better to give them a 'hello,' in passing and let them be. Don't have no conversation with mermaids and above all don't listen to them singing. It will muddle you."

"Thank you," said Galldora, "thank you very much, Mr Crab."

"You're welcome," mumbled the crab, as he walked away sideways.

"That was very kind of him," said Galldora out loud.

"Oh, was it?" snapped the mermaid. "I think it was most spiteful of that crab and he was just talking rubbish. Oh, do hurry up and think of something to keep the hair out of my eyes, my arms are aching, and I want to go and play!"

"I know," said Galldora, "I've got the very thing for you—my ribbon."

"Give it to me," said the mermaid, putting out a hand and letting half of her long hair fall down.

"Well, I can't exactly give it to you," answered Galldora sadly, "you will have to come and get it. I'm a doll, you see, and I can't walk."

The mermaid swam about on the edge of the waves and peered at the rag doll, and got very cross. She pouted and flicked her tail and then said, "I can't walk either, so we'll just have to wait for the sea to come up and wash you to me, that's all."

"Oh, I do hope not, what will become of me then?" gasped Galldora.

"Don't you like the sea?" asked the mermaid in surprise.

"No."

"That's funny, the sea is safe."

"Yes, to you, because you are a mermaid, but I'm a rag doll, and rag dolls find the sea very unsafe, I can assure you."

"What colour is your ribbon?" asked the mermaid, changing the subject.

"Blue," said Galldora.

"I like blue," said the mermaid.

"It's got a silver safety-pin holding the ribbon to my hair."

"What's a safety-pin like? I can't see."

"You've let your hair go all over your face again, that's why," said Galldora.

"Well, my arms were aching so," answered the mermaid. "Oh, I do wish the sea would hurry up and wash you out!"

"Do you think it really will?" gasped Galldora in alarm.

"Oh, yes, of course," answered the mermaid, "I know it will. It's still coming in, and your castle wall is slowly crumbling."

"If I am a good rag doll——" began Galldora, then she stopped. "Of course," she mumbled to herself, "it's the other way round with mermaids." So she started again. "If I am a bad rag doll and let you have my ribbon for keeps, and my safety-pin, will you be a bad mermaid in return and throw me out of the sea far behind the castle, where I will be safe."

"Oh, yes, all right," said the mermaid, "let's be bad together," which, of course, to the mermaid meant being good.

So when at last the sea broke through the castle walls and washed Galldora out the mermaid picked her up. The mermaid took her blue ribbon and the safety-pin, and then threw her over the crumbling castle on to the far dry sand.

"Thank you," shouted Galldora, lying on her back in the sand-dunes. "Does the ribbon work?" she called.

"Yes, rather," shouted back the mermaid, "I've tied some of my hair one side with the ribbon and pulled some of the other through the safety-pin. It's lovely. I can see now. I can go and play and play and play. I'll be able to play catch with the porpoises like I never did before, and grandmother's steps with the whales. What fun!"

Then, as the mermaid swam away singing, she turned just for a second and waved a last good-bye to the rag doll. Soon her song was lost in the song of the sea, and the silver flick of her silver tail was lost in the silver of the moon's light that spread upon the waters.

Galldora was found next day by Marybell, and Marybell knew at once that she must have had some strange adventure, for how else did the rag doll leave the sea-washed castle, and how did she lose her ribbon and the safety-pin?

"I hope it was a happy adventure," said Marybell to Galldora. Galldora's shoe-button eyes shone back so brightly that Marybell knew it had indeed been a very happy adventure, and she was glad.

Galldora and the Rooks

ONE WILD, WINDY DAY Galldora, the rag doll, was swung up into the air by Marybell. Up and up the wind carried Galldora, but she never came down, for Galldora fell *plomp* into an old rooks' nest. It was a thin old nest full of holes, and the rag doll settled right in the middle. Galldora looked down, and far below she saw the grass like a green sea, and Marybell far, far away.

"Oh!" said Galldora to herself. "Now what will become of me?"

"Never mind, Galldora," called up Marybell, "the twigs will soon break in this wind and you'll come falling down. I'll go away and have my tea now and come back for you later."

But Marybell forgot to come back. Anyway it would have been no good, for the twigs held and Galldora remained stuck in the old rooks' nest.

Next day two rooks came and looked at the rag doll.

"Aaaah!" said one.

"Aaaah!" said the other.

"Oh, go away, rooks," said Galldora. "Don't bother me. This is my home now and I'm happy here."

But the two rooks started pulling Galldora about. One pulled her arms while the other pulled her feet. But as they were both pulling in different ways, Galldora stayed where she was.

At last the rooks gave up. They hopped from branch to branch, flapping their wings and looking again at the rag doll. They looked at her this way, then they looked at her that way. Then one rook looked at her from above, and the other rook looked at her from below.

One rook called, "Floor."

"Aaaah!" called the other nodding its head. "Floor-floor."

They flew away, still calling "Floor-floor" to each other.

What do they mean? Galldora asked herself. She soon found out. They made her into a floor and built a new nest on top of her. After a few days she was covered with twigs, and only her head stuck up in the middle.

After a few more days there were five eggs in the nest. The mother rook sat on the eggs to keep them warm. When she flew off to find food Galldora kept the eggs warm with her wool hair.

One sunny day out of the five eggs, with a peck-peck, came five baby rooks.

"Aaaah! Aren't my babies bonny?" called the mother rook proudly.

If I was asked, said Galldora to herself, I would say I had never seen such ugly babies.

But though Galldora thought they were ugly, she took a great liking to the baby rooks, and she began to feel motherly towards them. At first she did not like the way they pecked her eyes and pulled at her hair, but she got used to it.

Then, after a while, the baby rooks grew so big that the nest seemed very crowded and much too small.

"I do wish they wouldn't sit on my head," said poor Galldora.

One night the wind started to blow. It blew in a wild way, and it bent and shook the high tree and the rooks' nest. The father and mother rook became very worried. They kept calling "Aaaah-aaaah!" to each other.

Whatever happens, said Galldora to herself, very firmly, I must not fall down, for if I fall the nest will come down too, and then what will happen to the baby rooks? And yet, added Galldora sadly, I would like to fall down. I am getting very tired of being up here. The baby rooks have grown so big, and the nest is getting very stuffy. Still, I must not be selfish and think about myself.

As the wind blew out the night stars and then blew in the dawn the rag doll began to feel very strange. Her legs had fallen down and only her arms held up the nest.

"Listen, baby rooks," she said. "Sit on

my arms and head, so that when I fall down you can float down with me."

The baby rooks did as Galldora said. With the last wild gust of wind Galldora fell, and the baby rooks, sitting on her, floated down. They fell on a soft flower-bed, Galldora first and the baby rooks on top of her.

The mother rook and father rook were so happy that their babies were safe, they gave Galldora acouple of sharp pecks with their beaks and said, "Aaah-aah!" in a thank you way.

The baby rooks were calling, "We can fly." And they started right away flapping their wings, and taking little flops from here to there.

Soon they were all safe on a low May-tree.

Later Marybell found Galldora. She gave her a hug, and said, "Why, Galldora, wherever have you been? I've been looking for you everywhere and I thought you were really lost for good this time." Marybell had quite forgotten that she had left Galldora in the tall tree.

Galldora and the Train Ride

ONE DAY MARYBELL took Galldora on a train ride. Marybell was going to have tea with her friend Jane. Jane lived in the small town of Tanminster, which was four miles away from Marybell's home. Marybell's mother rang up Jane's mother, and they decided that Marybell could be put on the train at Merryfields station by her mother, and Jane and Jane's mother would be waiting for her at Tanminster station.

Marybell was very excited.

"I'll take Galldora for company," she told her mother, "not one of my new dolls, because Galldora is so old it won't matter if the train soot gets all over her, and I think it will be very good for her education, don't you, Mummy?"

"Of course it will, dear," said Marybell's mother, "and remember Marybell, it's the next station."

So Marybell and Galldora were put on the train. It was a small train on a branch line.

When the train pulled up at Tanminster, Marybell got very muddled. "This doesn't look at all like the town where Jane lives," she told Galldora, "and I can't see Jane or her mummy anywhere."

In fact, there was no one on the station platform but the guard. Marybell tried to read the name of the station but she couldn't quite spell it out. She then thought of asking the guard. But it was too late. With a whistle from the guard and an answering whistle from the engine the train slowly rumbled on.

"It must have been a station Mummy forgot about," said Marybell.

Marybell did not know that Jane and Jane's mother arrived just as the train was moving out of the station. They thought Marybell had missed the train.

"Or perhaps she had a lift by car after all," said Jane.

"We'll go home and ring up," said Jane's mother.

When Jane's mother did ring up Marybell's mother was out.

In the train was Marybell with Galldora

propped up against the window to see the view. It was a wonderful sunny day, so sunny it was quite stuffy in the train.

I shall be very glad when we get out, thought Galldora. I am sure the sun will melt my shoe-button eyes.

The train went, "Sing-me-a-song—bump-me-along—sing-me-a-song," and the noise was so like a lullaby and the carriage was so warm and stuffy Marybell fell into a doze.

At last with a violent jerk they drew up at the next station.

Marybell woke up and jumped out of the train with Galldora. She stood on the platform for a moment, but there was neither Jane nor her mother. The guard had gone to join a friend in a small black shed for a cup of tea, as it was the last station on the small branch line. The engine was shunting down a side rail and getting ready to pull the train all the way back again. The man who took the tickets, thinking there were no tickets to take, had wandered up the platform, watering the flower-beds with a huge watering-can.

So Marybell and Galldora just walked out of the station. They wandered down a road, a strange road that neither of them had ever seen before. There were high trees on either side, and turtle doves were purring.

"I don't know where we are," said Marybell, "and I am getting very hungry."

Oh, dear! thought Galldora, how unfortunate.

There didn't seem to be any houses in sight, and the road went up and up a long hill and it grew darker and greener all the time.

Marybell got a stone in her sandal, so she had to sit at the side of the road, take off her sandal, and shake out the stone. When Marybell put her shoe on again and got up she quite forgot to pick up Galldora. Galldora lay at the side of the road and watched Marybell go on and on and on, and disappear round a bend. Galldora's shoe-button eyes grew very misty.

Life, said Galldora to herself, can be very sad. And she lay there, alone and forgotten, for a long time.

After an hour—it must have been quite an hour—a gipsy cart came by. A piebald pony was harnessed to an open cart, and in the cart were four children. The children's mother was driving the cart. They were coming down the hill.

"Mum! Mum!" shouted one of the children. "What's that, there, on the side—see?"

Now, gipsies are like squirrels, they can't bear to see anything just lying about. They have to go and pick it up and keep it. After all, everything comes in useful at one time or another. So the cart stopped, and Galldora was picked up.

"I want it!" shouted one of the children.

"It's mine—I saw it first, didn't I?" said the boy who had seen Galldora.

"Go on, give it to her," said an elder boy. "What do you want with a doll, anyway?" So

Galldora was taken and examined very thoroughly by the youngest gipsy child. Galldora's eyes were pulled and nearly came off. Galldora's hair was pulled, and some of it did come off.

"Dear me," sighed poor Galldora, "this is not at all nice. Still, I'm seeing life, and it's all good for my education."

The gipsies soon passed the station. But they didn't stop. On went the gipsy cart for quite a while and then it turned off the road.

Galldora found herself being taken out of the cart by her new owner. Soon she was seated down by a gipsy fire. Round the fire were three men—one older man and two young men. The young men were very gay. Their clothes were newish, and the handkerchiefs round their necks were brightly coloured; and their hats were set at a jaunty angle. The older man had a faded but still dashing look about him. A greyhound was sitting by his feet.

As soon as the greyhound saw Galldora he started to ripple all his muscles, and pointed out his long, thin snout to sniff. Then the greyhound slowly started to rise, but the man shouted, "Get down, there," and the animal sank down again.

"Well, thank goodness for that," said Galldora.

The woman, whose gold ear-rings flashed in the firelight, put a great saucepan on the flames. Her hair and her apron were as black as Galldora's eyes. Looking at her, Galldora thought how handsome she looked.

"I'm very glad now that my eyes are black," said Galldora, "because I can see that black is a very becoming colour."

Galldora was not left long to sit and gaze ahead. A little bantam cock came strutting up. He stood on one foot and stared at Galldora with one eye. The three wives of the bantam cock, all chatting at once, kept saying, "What is it? Is it good to eat? Let's have a go."

"Keep back," ordered the bantam cock, "and let me try first." He came and took a peck at Galldora and said, "Quite disgusting," and with that he turned his beautiful plumed tail on Galldora and strutted away. The wives, after casting a disapproving look at Galldora, hurried after the cock.

Then, when no one was looking, Galldora was pounced on by a puppy. The puppy was clearly a puppy of no pedigree and no finer feelings, for he tossed and worried poor

Galldora quite terribly. His teeth were sharp, and his claws were sharp too. Galldora thought lovingly of Marybell's spaniel, Sparks, for Sparks had a soft mouth and, though he loved to play with Galldora, he did it more in a pretending way than a real way.

Still, thought Galldora, we can't always expect an easy life, and she put up with the puppy's excited bitings and scratchings in a very gallant way. At last the puppy was thrown a bone, which he found more to his liking than Galldora, and he ran away, leaving Galldora very near the great fire.

Poor Galldora was nearly burned. Her dress and one side of her head was quite singed. As she lay there, Galldora thought of Marybell. I do hope she has found something to eat, Galldora kept on thinking.

Marybell had. Marybell was very happy. She was sitting up at a large table. Spread before her was cream and a honeycomb and lots of butter and scones, and a soft boiled egg, and ham.

"This is just the kind of meal I like best," Marybell was saying between each mouthful.

Sitting opposite Marybell was a small, wrinkled old lady. She looked exactly like a stored-away Cox's apple that was forgotten

in an attic. The old lady kept on looking at Marybell and saying, "Well, I don't know what to do for the best, I'm sure."

On the floor by the kitchen range was a little tabby cat and, playing by her, were two kittens with very tabby markings and very blue eyes. In the window was a round-looking wire cage, and in the cage sat a very moth-eaten-looking parrot. And every time the little old lady said "I don't know what to do for the best, I'm sure," the parrot whistled *Pop goes the Weasel.*

He whistled it very well, but he just couldn't get the end bit right, which seemed to worry him. He would pause a moment and then say, "Me-ow," just like the cats.

"If it wasn't for me rheumatics," at last said the little old lady, "I'd know what to do, but there—I'm a martyr to 'em."

"I like it here," said Marybell, who always liked other people's houses. Marybell looked at the window-sill and said, "I think you are very clever to grow a beautitful red flower like that."

"Ah, that's me cactus, love, and it likes the warm as I do."

"Up and down the City Road," sang the parrot.

Marybell helped herself to a huge slice of cherry-cake.

As Marybell was munching her fourth bit of cake, and the little old lady was saying, still staring at Marybell, "I wish I knew what to do for the best, I do, really." Marybell's daddy, a very worried, grey-looking daddy, was standing by the gipsy fire.

"No, sir," the older of the gipsy men was saying, "we've seen no girl hereabouts. Not to-day, have we, Vi?" The gipsy woman called Vi shook her head till her ear-rings rattled.

Marybell's daddy let his eyes wander to the cart. The gipsies had made a kind of hidden room under the cart by draping a waterproof cloth over the edges. The gipsy woman, noticing Marybell's daddy gazing at the improvised room, laughed.

"You don't think I'd keep her if I found her, do you, sir?" she said. "I've got enough of my own."

"Oh, well," said Marybell's daddy, "I'd better drive back to the station."

"She couldn't have gone farther than here, the train goes no farther," said one of the young men.

"I know," said Marybell's daddy. He was very dispirited. Just then the puppy caught sight of Galldora's eyes sparkling in the firelight. He pounced and dragged Galldora out.

"What have you got?" called one of the young men. All eyes were turned on the puppy and Galldora.

"Why!" cried Marybell's daddy excitedly, "that's her doll!"

The young man took Galldora away from the puppy and handed it to Marybell's daddy.

"Yes," said Marybell's daddy, "this is her doll, Galldora. I'd know her anywhere."

"We found it up on the hill, past the station," said the gipsy woman.

"You couldn't show me where that was exactly?" asked Marybell's daddy.

"One of the kids will go along with you, sir," said the gipsy woman, "he'd be pleased to have a ride in a car, and he can walk home."

But all four gipsy children wanted to go, so the four children and the puppy and Galldora went in the car.

The car stopped where Galldora had been found, and the gipsy children and the puppy got out. Marybell's daddy gave them a shilling each, which pleased them, and they waved him on his way with large friendly grins.

The car went on up the hill and round the bend till it came to a small cottage. It was a tiny, two-roomed cottage standing all alone, in a kind of lost way, at the side of the road. In the window was a parrot in a cage and a giant cactus, with a huge red cactus-flower. Marybell's daddy knocked at the door.

"Come in," called a high, thin voice, and Marybell's daddy went in. At first he could hardly see, for the heat of the room seemed to sting his eyes, and then he could hardly see because he was being hugged so much.

"I'm so glad you've come," said Marybell, "because I was just beginning to be lost, and Mrs Robins and I were wondering what to do for the best."

Marybell's daddy was so happy at finding Marybell that he quite forgot to scold her. He thanked little old Mrs Robins, who said, "Marybell must come for tea again one day."

Then Marybell climbed into her daddy's car and was driven home. Marybell was very tired, and fell asleep in the car, but before she fell asleep she said, "I'm glad I'm found and I promise I'll never go for a train ride on my own again."

"You'd better thank Galldora," said Marybell's daddy, "for if it hadn't been for her I might not have found you for a very long time."

"Galldora's a very clever doll," said Marybell, hugging Galldora. "She's my very favourite doll, although she's so old."

It's all this travelling that has made me clever, thought Galldora to herself. My education is coming on very well, I think, but all the same, I'm very glad, Marybell is not going to take me for a train ride all by herself again. It gave me quite a fright.

Galldora's Holiday

ONE DAY MARYBELL washed her rag doll, Galldora, and hung her on the washing line to dry. It was a breezy sort of day and Galldora dried quickly.

But oh, dear! When Galldora was dry she did look pale. Her red cheeks had gone, her wool hair was lank, and even her shoe-button eyes had become dull.

Marybell had a long think. There seemed to be only one thing to do. Galldora must have a holiday. But where? It was when they were in the park that Marybell decided the park would be a lovely holiday place.

So Marybell left Galldora sitting up against a notice which read: *Keep off the grass.*

"You must sunbathe and have lots of fresh air," Marybell told Galldora, "and I'll come back and fetch you."

"Where's Galldora?" asked Marybell's

KEEP OFF
THE GRASS

mother that evening as she tucked Marybell up in bed. "Has she got lost again?"

"No, I know where she is," answered Marybell, cheerfully.

Meanwhile in the park Galldora was quite enjoying herself. She watched the ducks which always made her laugh.

Then Mr Ferguson saw her.

Now Mr Ferguson was the head park keeper. He lived in a small house at the edge of the park, and all day long he walked about the park in a very bad temper.

So you see, when Mr Ferguson saw Galldora sitting on his tidy grass against his notice which read: *Keep off the grass*, he made a growling noise inside his throat which frightened Galldora.

Then Mr Ferguson picked up Galldora and took her to his small house.

Mrs Ferguson, his wife, was very shocked when she saw Galldora.

"What a washed-out doll' " she said. "Poor thing."

And at once she started to make Galldora a new dress, and she stitched on new hair, and she polished up her eyes, and she even gave her rosy cheeks. Then she sat Galldora by the window and talked to her.

When Marybell came to fetch Galldora and found she was really lost, she was just about to cry, when she stopped, for Mr Ferguson was shouting, *"Keep off my grass."*

Now usually Marybell was frightened of Mr Ferguson, but today she was very brave, and told Mr Ferguson why she was on his grass, and all about Galldora.

To Marybell's surprise Mr Ferguson smiled.

"Oh, so that's her name. Well, I shall be sorry to part with Galldora, and so will my wife. We have grown so fond of her."

He took Marybell to meet his wife and fetch Galldora.

Marybell was delighted to see Galldora looking so bonny, and Galldora was delighted to be going home. But she had to admit that she had had an interesting holiday, and was pleased to have made friends with such important people as Mr and Mrs Ferguson, head keepers of the park.

Galldora and the Kittens

JAMIE, THE BOY FROM the house next door to Marybell's house, had a charming tabby cat with black paws. She was called Lancing.

Now Lancing became a mother-cat and had five kittens. They were funny little things, with their eyes tightly closed. But Lancing was very proud of them. And so was Jamie. He showed the kittens to everyone.

His mummy said, "You know, Jamie, if you go on showing the kittens to everyone, Lancing will take them away and hide them."

"Why?" asked Jamie.

"Because cats are very good mothers and they like to bring up their kittens in their own way and they don't like them being shown to everyone until they are quite big kittens."

After that Jamie did try not to pick up the kittens and show them to everyone. But he didn't think Lancing would mind if he showed them to Marybell every time Marybell came to play.

Well, Lancing did mind. And she decided to hide her kittens.

Lancing peeped this way and that and found no-one was about, no-one except Galldora.

Marybell had left Galldora on guard, while she and Jamie went into the garden to play.

Suddenly, to Galldora's alarm, Lancing stopped peeping about and picked up one of the kittens very gently with her mouth and carried it away.

Then Lancing came back for another kitten, and another, and another.

"Oh! dear," thought Galldora. "I'll be blamed for this, for I'm on guard."

When the last kitten had gone, do you know what happened? Lancing came back, picked Galldora up in her mouth very gently, and carried her away, too.

She carried Galldora upstairs, out of a window, along a low roof and into a small hole, to a dark, warm place.

"I believe we must be in part of the attic that is boarded off," thought Galldora.

Lancing dropped Galldora beside her other kittens.

Quite a few days went by and Galldora got very fond of the kittens who grew up fast. They opened their eyes and even toddled about. They bumped into each other and into Galldora, just as if she were also a kitten.

Then one day the biggest kitten dragged Galldora out of the warm place on to the roof.

"There, now," thought Galldora, "he's going to fall off. He's very wobbly on his legs."

But he didn't fall off. It was Galldora who fell. She fell on to Jamie's head. Jamie looked up to the roof and saw the kitten.

"So that's where Lancing hid the kittens," he said, and ran into the house to tell his mummy.

Marybell, who was standing beside Jamie, picked up Galldora and gave her a hug. "I thought this time you were lost for ever, and I'm so glad you're not, and thank you for guarding the kittens and showing us where they were hidden."

And Marybell smiled at Galldora and Galldora smiled back.

Galldora goes to School

ONE DAY WHEN MARYBELL was all ready to go to school she picked up her rag doll, Galldora, and said: "I think you'd better come to school with me, Galldora, because you're getting stupider and stupider, and if you sit with me at school and listen to the teacher you might learn something."

So Marybell pushed Galldora into her satchel, and off they went with Marybell's mother to the school.

At the end of the road where Marybell lived was a little shop that sold almost everything, and beyond the shop was the main road. This went to the big shops, and the supermarkets, and the hairdressers, and the library, and to Marybell's school.

The school wasn't too far away. In fact, it came before the big shops, but as it was on the main road Marybell's mother always took

Marybell to school, and fetched her home again after school.

Galldora knew that Marybell liked school, so she was really looking forward to her day there.

After Marybell had taken off her hat and coat she picked Galldora out of her satchel and took her into the class-room.

The schoolteacher, who was called Miss Wiggins—and generally "Miss"—was very pleased to meet Galldora. She had heard a lot about her. So she thought it would be a very good idea if Galldora sat on a table near to her. She propped Galldora up against a large jar full of bright leaves and colourful berries.

At first Galldora was very interested in watching the children dance to music and pretending to be animals. But as the morning went on Galldora got very sleepy.

"I suppose I just *must* be stupid," she told herself, "but I do find all this learning very tiring."

Soon she fell asleep, and rolled off the table behind a pile of drawing-paper and books.

Suddenly the lights were switched on, and Galldora woke up with a start.

A man with a bushy beard who was looking through the papers on the floor saw Galldora, and picked her up.

"Hullo!" he said in a very friendly way. "Some little girl must have lost you." He propped Galldora up again, against the jar full of coloured leaves and berries.

"There," he said, "That will make an interesting picture to paint."

Galldora was very surprised to see that there were no children in the class-room any more, but only grown-ups. All the grown-ups had easels and paint-boxes, and they settled down and started to paint the jar of coloured leaves and berries—and Galldora!

After the class was over the art teacher—who was the man with the bushy beard—pinned a letter on to Galldora, and all the grown-ups went home.

The next day "Miss" read the letter out to Marybell's class. The note said: "Will the little girl who owns this doll which she lost, please lend her to us to paint for the Tuesday evening grown-ups' painting class? This doll has a most interesting and intelligent face. Of course, we will take great care of her."

Marybell wasn't quite sure about lending Galldora to grown-ups. But Miss Wiggins, the teacher, told Marybell that she knew the grown-ups' art teacher very well. He was called Mr Laurence, and she knew that Mr Laurence would take great care of Galldora. So Marybell said "yes."

"And I think that *you* can all try painting Galldora, too," said "Miss."

Galldora was very pleased.

"That's because I've got such an intelligent face," she told herself, "but this time I must try to keep awake."

Please Shut the Gate

BOTH MARYBELL AND HER rag doll Galldora loved going out for a picnic, so they were very happy when Marybell's mother said one day: "I want to go and see Auntie Daisy, and Daddy's promised to drive us there in the car, so we'll have a picnic lunch on the way."

"Oh, how lovely, mummy!" said Marybell. "Can I bring Galldora because she loves picnics, too?"

"Of course you can," answered Marybell's mother, and she added: "Would you like to ask Jamie to come along with us, Marybell? He'll be company for you, as it's a very long drive."

"Well, I don't know if I want Jamie to come with us," said Marybell. "You see, I'm not talking to Jamie at the moment, because he's not being at all friendly. He won't let me have a turn on his new two-wheeler bike."

"I'm sure he will when the bicycle isn't quite so new," said Marybell's mother, "so run along and ask Jamie if he'd like to come with us."

"Oh, all *right*," said Marybell, "and I suppose he'll say 'Yes' because he likes picnics as much as Galldora and I do."

It was a lovely morning when they all set off in Marybell's father's car to see Auntie Daisy . . . And indeed everything went very well until the picnic was over.

They had eaten their picnic in a field. On the gate was a notice which said PLEASE CLOSE THIS GATE.

Marybell's father explained that cows were always very curious, and if the gate was open they would come outside the field to explore, and get lost.

There was not much grass in the meadow because the cows had eaten it right down, and one cow was looking over the fence at the green grass growing on the other side.

When the picnic was over and packed away Marybell and Jamie and Galldora went to have a last walk in the fields, looking for mushrooms.

PLEASE
SHUT THE

Suddenly the cows started running towards them. This rather frightened Jamie and Marybell, and they ran out of the meadow and FORGOT to close the gate properly. What's more, Marybell forgot Galldora whom she had left lying in the grass.

Marybell and Jamie jumped into the car, and they all drove away.

The cows didn't go out of the gate, because they saw Galldora. And of course, being curious they came and stared down at her.

"What are you?" asked one of the cows.

"My name is Galldora, and if you don't mind, please try not to trample on me."

"Oh, we wouldn't do that," said the cows, who were really very polite. "We're just going out of the gate, anyway, to find some green grass to eat."

Now Galldora knew that if they did this they would get lost, because she had heard Marybell's father say so.

"I must keep them here," thought Galldora, and she did. She chatted away to them, and the cows thought she was very amusing. They were still standing around her when the car came back because Marybell found that Galldora had got lost again.

Then Marybell was very brave. She ran into the field before anyone could stop her, and she RESCUED Galldora.

"Do you know, Marybell," said Jamie on their way back from seeing Auntie Daisy, "you were so brave with those cows that I think you'd be brave enough to try and ride my two-wheeler."

And next day both Marybell and Galldora had turns on Jamie's new two-wheeler bike.

Galldora becomes an Actress

MARYBELL AND JAMIE, THE boy next door, were great friends. So when Jamie's father made Jamie a swing under a branch of their walnut tree, Jamie asked Marybell to come over and try it before they went to school.

Marybell loved swinging so much that she begged Jamie to let her show Galldora, her rag doll, what fun it was.

"All right," said Jamie, "but be careful, because you must hold on with both hands. Just let Galldora sit in your lap, or else you might fall off."

Marybell tucked her feet under her and then pushed them out, and swung higher and higher with Galldora in her lap. Then suddenly when Marybell was high in the air—*whizz*—Galldora flew out of her lap right over the hedge and into Mr Crake's garden.

Now both Marybell and Jamie knew that Mr Crake didn't like children. So when Marybell got off the swing she stared at the fence and sobbed, "Oh, Jamie, what shall we do? Mr Crake will never give Galldora back."

"I'll go and fetch her," said Jamie bravely, and he climbed through the hole in the fence and into Mr Crake's garden. But though he searched and searched he couldn't find Galldora anywhere.

Galldora was lost.

Now it wasn't surprising that Jamie couldn't find Galldora, because this is what had happened. Just as Galldora came flying through the air Mr Crake was driving out of his garage, and Galldora fell—PLONK—on to the roof-rack of the car.

When Mr Crake arrived at his office and got out of his car he saw Galldora on the roof. He fetched her down and flung her roughly into the back seat, saying, "Children! Really! They're just a nuisance!"

Galldora spent all day alone in the car.

When the office was closed Mr Crake came out and got into his car, but he didn't drive straight home. He drove to the Town Hall where an amateur theatrical show was about to begin.

Mr Crake was not an amateur actor, but he played the 'cello, and he had come to play it in the orchestra. He ignored Galldora, took his 'cello from the boot of the car and went into the Town Hall.

What a fuss there was in the Town Hall, because a doll who was a very important part of the play hadn't turned up, and the audience was beginning to arrive.

Mr Crake remembered Galldora.

"I've got a rag doll in my car," he told the Producer of the play.

"Then please fetch her at once, Mr Crake, I beg of you," said the Producer.

So, to Galldora's great surprise she became an actress. This was very exciting, and she loved being on the stage. She found all the actors and actresses so kind and helpful. But when the show was over, and the audience had stopped clapping, and everybody started to go home, Galldora felt very sad.

"I do hope Mr Crake remembers me," she thought, "I wouldn't like to be left here all lost and forgotten."

Mr Crake *did* remember and put Galldora back in his car. Next morning he took her round to Marybell.

"I suppose," said Mr Crake, "it's too much to ask you to teach Galldora not to get lost in my garden. But I'll forgive her this time as she was most helpful." Then he told Marybell what a wonderful actress Galldora had been.

"You're a very clever doll," Marybell told Galldora, "but please don't get conceited and get lost again in Mr Crake's garden."

Galldora and the Hedgehog

EVEN WITH HIS BEST PAIR of glasses on, Mr Sparrow didn't see very clearly, and when he had to use his second pair of glasses because he had broken his good pair he could hardly see at all. So it wasn't surprising that when Mr Sparrow was tidying up Jamie's garden in the autumn, wearing his second pair, he thought that Galldora who was lying on the path was only an old bundle of rags tied together with string.

"That'll come in useful," said Mr Sparrow to himself, "just right to help the bonfire," and he carried Galldora to the unlit bonfire at the end of the garden. Then a little while later he threw a whole pile of garden clippings and weedings ON TOP of Galldora.

Galldora was very alarmed. "I don't think Marybell will ever find me now," she thought sadly to herself. Indeed, Galldora grew sadder

and sadder as the morning went on, because Mr Sparrow would keep piling more and more weeds and garden clippings on top of her.

Then Mr Sparrow stood by his bonfire, wetted his finger and held it up to see which way the wind was blowing.

"The smoke will blow nicely away from the house," murmured Mr Sparrow, and he was just about to light his bonfire when Mr Crake popped his head over the fence and said: "Mr Sparrow, if you light that bonfire I'll have to complain. The smoke will come straight into my house and garden."

Mr Sparrow and Mr Crake had quite a few words after that, and at last Mr Sparrow agreed to wait until the wind changed. But he went away mumbling: "I'll light it tomorrow, which-ever way the wind blows."

That evening when all the garden was still Galldora heard a scuffle-scuffling noise. Gall-dora looked about as best she could, and there was a hedgehog grunting and snuffling, and snuffling and grunting, and making a tunnel into the bonfire.

"Hi, there!" called Galldora, "what are you up to?"

The hedgehog took no notice of her and refused to answer until he was comfortably tucked up near her.

"*Now, please don't talk*," said the hedgehog, "I'm feeling very sleepy, though I don't know why. But I seem to get sleepier and sleepier every day."

And the hedgehog went fast asleep.

"Poor creature," thought Galldora, "it does seem *very* tired out." But Galldora found it very difficult to go on feeling motherly because the hedgehog started to snore. And *did* he snore!

"It's very unfriendly of him," thought Galldora. "Even a Doll needs forty winks, and I'm certainly not going to get them now."

So Galldora was very pleased when the robin sang in the dawn, and woke up the blackbird. Then the blackbird sang so loudly that he woke up all the other birds, and that woke up the hedgehog.

"Aaaah, breakfast time," said the hedgehog, and started scuffling out of the bonfire. And as he scuffled his prickles caught Galldora's hair, so that she was pulled right out of Mr Sparrow's rubbish heap and on to the path.

Luckily, Mr Sparrow's best glasses had been

mended, and he was wearing them that morning when he came to light the bonfire. He saw Galldora lying in the middle of the path.

"Now, then, however did you get there?" he asked. "Your Marybell's been looking everywhere for you."

He picked Galldora up, and carried her next door to Marybell.

Galldora at the Hairdressers

MARYBELL LOVED GOING TO the hairdressers with her mother, for the long hairdressing room was warm and lovely-smelling and the mirrors were so shiny bright, and the hairdressing ladies were always smiling and happy.

Marybell didn't even mind having her hair trimmed, but she didn't have it washed like her mother, for her mother liked to wash Marybell's hair herself.

Now one day the long room was so crowded that all the hairdressing ladies were too busy even to smile.

"I'm glad I brought Galldora to play with and my book to look at," Marybell told her mother, "because I think we will have to wait a long time before your hair is washed and dried and mine is trimmed."

"I'm afraid you will," answered her mother.

The room was so crowded there wasn't even a chair for Marybell to sit on, so she sat on a cushion on the floor, and she and Galldora looked at the book.

After a while a hairdressing lady told Marybell she could come now to the tall chair by one of the mirrors to have her hair trimmed.

Marybell jumped up leaving Galldora and her book on the floor. She thought Galldora would be all right. And perhaps Galldora would have been all right if that naughty little boy Ian hadn't seen her.

Now Ian knew Marybell and Galldora, but he didn't take Galldora back to Marybell. Oh, no, he took Galldora to the far end of the long room. Even though Ian was only four he shouldn't have done that, should he?

Then Ian saw a bright shining pair of scissors on the floor and he picked them up. And do you know what he did? HE CUT OFF GALLDORA'S HAIR!

"Oh! no," thought poor Galldora, "and I was rather proud of my black wool hair, and now I'LL LOOK A FREAK!"

"All smart," said Ian.

But when he looked at Galldora with her hair cut off he got frightened and he dropped her, and ran down the long room to find his mother.

Ian's mother was talking to Marybell's mother. They were all ready to go home and Marybell was looking for her book and Galldora. She found her book but no Galldora. Ian had been watching and he said, "Galldora's lost."

Marybell nearly cried. But Ian's mother said,

"I think Ian knows where Galldora is, don't you, Ian? Where is she, Ian?"

"Galldora—all smart," was all Ian would say.

A kind hairdressing lady found Galldora and brought her to Marybell. But when Marybell saw Galldora with hardly any hair, she burst into tears.

"Don't cry, dear," said the kind hairdressing lady. "I'll give your doll a lovely new hairstyle."

And she did. She trimmed and brushed and fluffed up Galldora's hair. And she showed Galldora her new hairstyle in the mirror.

"Yes," thought Galldora, "that is rather a becoming new hairstyle, though I don't look quite myself."

But Galldora, being a kind-hearted doll, forgave Ian because he really did think he was making her smart when he cut her hair off.

Marybell forgave him, too.

Galldora and the Doll's House

ONE DAY MRS PEARLBRIGHT took Marybell and Galldora and Jamie and Ian and Angela for a whole day's outing in her large car. She took Ian's mother as well to help her look after the children.

"Where are we going?" asked Marybell.

"It's a mystery drive," answered Mrs Pearlbright, "so you'll just have to wait and see."

At the end of the mystery drive they arrived at a large 'Stately Home'.

"My," thought Galldora when she saw the house, "a very grand person must live here."

But in fact nobody lived in the house, though everything was arranged just as if somebody did. There were rooms and rooms full of tables and chairs and mirrors and pictures on the walls, and curtains at the windows.

"I'm getting bored," said Marybell after a while.

"So am I," said Jamie.

Angela who was ahead of them called out. "Marybell, Jamie, come and look, there are lots of dolls' houses here and stuffed birds."

So Marybell, Galldora, Jamie, and Ian went to have a look and there down a long corridor were seven dolls' houses and cases of stuffed birds.

Jamie liked the birds best but Marybell and Angela were fascinated with the dolls' houses. After a time they joined Jamie looking at the birds. Ian liked the dolls' houses too, and he didn't join the others but went and sat on the floor by one of the dolls' houses and he fidgeted and fidgeted with the catch until he broke it and the front opened. Ian was delighted. Then do you know WHAT HE DID? He picked up Galldora and SQUEEZED her into the staircase.

I am sure he meant to take Galldora out again, but just then Mrs Pearlbright called, "Coooeee, children . . . time to go and get some tea." Ian was the first to run away from the corridor and the others followed.

And there was poor Galldora lost and forgotten, feeling like a giant. Her head was on the second floor, and her feet were in the hall.

"I'm so sorry," she said to the occupants of the house, "please forgive me."

"Granted," said the man of the house.

Suddenly Galldora began to slip and as she slipped her hair got tangled up in a chair, and everything started tumbling about.

"Why," said the lady of the doll's house, "there's our Billy. He's been hiding all these years behind that piano. What a kind giant you are to find our little boy again."

That made Galldora feel better, but she did hope that Marybell would discover she was lost and come and find her, because she found being a giant in a doll's house was not a very pleasant experience.

After tea Marybell did miss Galldora, and when Ian told them where Galldora was lost, they all went to the dolls' houses. Mrs Pearlbright tied up the doll's house and put little Billy by his mother. "Galldora's done a good deed by getting lost in this doll's house," said Mrs Pearlbright, "because it was in a higgledy-piggledy mess and now it's all trim and tidy."

Galldora was sure, as Marybell carried her away, that the occupants of the doll's house all waved her a "Thank you".

Who Put Her In?

"CAN I CLEAN YOUR windows, Mr Crake?" asked Jamie hopefully.

"No," answered Mr Crake.

"It's for a good cause. We are all working to get money for the old people's outing. Perhaps you could go too, Mr Crake."

"I'm not an old person yet," said Mr Crake.

"Well, could I weed your path?"

"Oh, very well," answered Mr Crake. "Here's 50p and be careful not to weed out the flowers."

"Oh, thanks, Mr Crake, I'll go and get a basket and a fork and some help."

Mr Crake nodded and went back into his house.

Jamie got Marybell to help him, and Marybell brought Galldora. They had to bring Ian as well for, though Ian wouldn't be any help, as he was only four, he was visiting Marybell

while his mother went shopping.

Jamie and Marybell worked very hard pulling out the weeds and they left Ian to amuse himself.

And Ian did, for when they weren't looking he picked up Galldora and took her to a well he had found and threw her in. Then he sang: "Galldora's in the well. Who threw her in? Ian did, Ian did. Who'll pull her out?" Then he went away.

"Who IS going to pull you out?" asked a voice in the well.

"Oh, dear me," gasped Galldora, "I didn't know anyone else was down here."

"Well, there is. There's me, Bumps."

"If you don't mind me asking, Bumps," said Galldora as politely as she could, "and as I can't see very clearly down here, what are you?"

"I'm not a what, I'm a who. I'm a toad, a real toad, not like this well. It's artificial, you know, not all that deep and only a puddle of rain water in it."

"Going down wells has been left out of my education up till now," said Galldora, "so I wouldn't know. But I do hope that little boy Ian will tell my Marybell where I am, otherwise I'll be really and truly lost."

"Pity," said Bumps, "you being lost, for I had hoped to ask a favour of you, that is, when you are pulled out. It's this . . . Could I possibly sit on your head and be pulled up with you? I'm tired of living down here."

"Of course," said Galldora. She was pleased to have Bumps to talk to, for it stopped her worrying about being lost.

Later when Marybell discovered that Galldora had completely disappeared she started to cry. Then Ian started to sing at the top of his voice: "Pussy's down the well . . . who put her in?"

Suddenly Mr Crake came into the garden

and said: "What on earth is all this noise about?"

Jamie explained, and Ian went on singing, "Pussy's in the well."

"In the well? Ah!" said Mr Crake, "I wonder . . . ?" He went to the well and looked down and saw Galldora. Then he lowered a bucket and scooped Galldora up . . . with Bumps sitting on her head.

"Thanks for the lift up," said Bumps as he hopped away.

"It was a pleasure," answered Galldora. But poor Mr Crake's trousers—they were covered with muddy water.

"Take that doll home at once," ordered Mr Crake, "and don't let her get lost in my garden again."

"I'll try not," answered Marybell, "I promise." But Galldora is the strangest doll—she's always getting lost.

Galldora's Box of Fireworks

"I'M GOING TO HAVE A fireworks party on Guy Fawkes Night," Jamie told Marybell. "We're going to have baked potatoes cooked in the ashes of the bonfire, and my Daddy's doing the fireworks. Everyone's coming, and you'll come, of course, won't you, Marybell?"

Marybell was a bit frightened of fireworks, so she said quickly, "Galldora doesn't like fireworks. They scare her. So I'll have to stay at home to keep her company."

"Gracious me!" thought Galldora, who was listening. "I didn't know I was scared of fireworks."

But the day before the fireworks party Galldora got lost, and so did William Bird, the budgerigar who belonged to Mr and Mrs Newman of Willow Lane Stores. He was a happy little bird, and always said, "Want a cup of tea?" to anyone who talked to him.

On the morning of the fireworks party Marybell went shopping for her mother at Willow Lane Stores, and Mrs Newman told Marybell about her lost budgie.

"You see, dear, I always let him play outside his cage every evening. Yesterday a firework went off so near that I ran outside to see if any damage had been done to the shop windows, and I quite forgot to close the back door. And poor William was so frightened of the fireworks that he flew right out of the house. If you do see a lost budgie, you will tell me, won't you dear?"

"Yes, of course I will," said Marybell, "and if you see my Galldora you'll tell me, won't you?"

"Of course, dear," said Mrs Newman.

"You see, *she's* frightened of fireworks banging, like your budgie William, and I'm sure that's why she's got lost."

Now, as Marybell was on her way home, walking very slowly because the shopping-basket was heavy, she DID SEE a budgerigar. He was sitting on a pile of wet, swept-up leaves just outside somebody's front gate.

Marybell stopped and put down her shopping-basket. Then she walked very quietly towards the budgie, saying, "Good boy, William, I won't hurt you." The budgie flapped his wings, and tried to fly away, but he couldn't.

"He's hurt," thought Marybell, "I'll have to run back to the shop and tell Mr and Mrs Newman."

Mr Newman came AT ONCE. There was William, the budgie, just as before, sitting on the wet leaves. And just as before he tried to fly away, but couldn't. Mr Newman very gently put his hand over the little bird, and lifted him. And as he did so OUT CAME GALLDORA from under the leaves.

"Galldora!" gasped Marybell. "So that's where you've been lost!"

"Well I never," said Mr Newman, "one of William's claws is all tangled up in that necklace round your doll's neck. How very clever of Galldora to catch him like that."

William was so happy to be back in his own cage that he chirped at once: "Want a cup of tea?"

"Thank you, dear, for telling us about our budgie," said Mrs Newman, and Mr Newman said, "Galldora shall have a reward. She shall have a box of fireworks, and I'll bring them

round when I shut up shop at five o'clock."

When the box of fireworks arrived Marybell said, "Jamie had better have them for his party." So she, and Galldora, and her daddy took them round to Jamie. And the party was such fun, and the bonfire was so bright, that Marybell stayed and enjoyed herself after all.

While Galldora—just in case she got frightened of the bangs—stayed inside Jamie's house and watched her own lovely colourful fireworks through the window.

Galldora and the Wrong Shopping-basket

MARYBELL LOVED TO GO shopping for her mother. So when Marybell's mother hadn't time to go to the supermarket for this or that which she had forgotten to buy she let Marybell go to the shop on the corner, and do the shopping for her. The corner shop was at the far end of the road where Marybell lived, just before the busy main road, so it was quite safe for Marybell to go there by herself.

And it was a most useful shop because Mr and Mrs Newman kept a little of everything in it—like sweets and gumboots, paraffin, bread, notepaper, post cards, fresh fruit and tinned fruit, and ice-cream, cleaning things, dusters and brushes, and even a few medicines. The only things they didn't keep were fresh fish and fresh meat.

Now one day when Marybell went shopping at Willow Lane Stores she lost Galldora. Marybell couldn't think *how* she lost Galldora, but really it was quite simple. Galldora was popped into the WRONG basket, for Miss Pettywin's basket was EXACTLY like Marybell's. While Mr Newman was serving Marybell

Mrs Newman was serving Miss Pettywin. The baskets were side by side on the counter with Galldora between them, and silly Mr Newman put Galldora into Miss Pettywin's basket.

Of course Miss Pettywin was very surprised when she got home and found in her basket under a lot of bread and sugar and things—Galldora.

"Well I never," said Miss Pettywin, "Well I *never*!" and she sat Galldora between some pot-plants in her sunny kitchen window.

Now Miss Pettywin lived all alone and was a very, very tidy person. She hadn't one speck of dust anywhere. Everything in her house was shining and polished.

"Dear me," said Miss Pettywin after she had put all her shopping away into cupboards, "I thought I'd bought a mop head, but I suppose that little girl in the shop got my mop head in her basket, and I got her rag doll. Well now, that is a nuisance because I've thrown my old mop head away and I must polish my floors."

Then she looked at Galldora. "Aha," she said, "I'm sure you won't mind helping me out, rag doll, and I think you can. You'll make a splendid polisher."

"I don't mind helping," thought Galldora,

"but I'm not sure how I could be a polisher."

She soon found out, for Miss Pettywin took Galldora off the window-sill and fetched out a couple of dusters. Then she tied the yellow dusters up with Galldora doubled up in the middle. Then she set to work. She put on her apron, and with Galldora in the dusters she polished and polished all her bright, shiny floors.

Then she untied the dusters, gave Galldora a good shake and sat her among the pot-plants again.

"Thank you," she said, "for helping me out. Now I think we'll have a cup of tea."

Next day Miss Pettywin went down to Willow Lane Stores with Galldora in her basket, and there in the shop was Marybell with the mop head in her basket.

So they exchanged.

"I'm ever so sorry," said Marybell, "but Galldora just seems to like getting lost."

"She was very helpful, my dear, very helpful indeed," said Miss Pettywin, and as a "thank you" she bought Marybell an ice-cream and Galldora a bag of Dolly Mixture sweets.